ENGINEERING
IRELAND

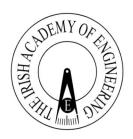

EDITED BY
RONALD COX

The Collins Press

Published in 2006 by
The Collins Press
West Link Park
Doughcloyne
Wilton
Cork

British Library Cataloguing in Publication Data

Engineering Ireland
      1. Engineering - Ireland - History
      2. Engineers - Ireland
      I. Cox, Ronald C.
      624'.09415

      ISBN-10: 1905172060
      ISBN-13: 978-1905172061

Book design and typesetting: Anú Design, Tara
Font: Caslon 11pt
Printed in Spain

This publication has received support from the Heritage Council under the 2006 Publications Grant Scheme.

CONTENTS

Part III · Construction and Public Works

Part IV · Energy and Industry

CONTRIBUTORS

P. Finbar Callanan, BE, MAI (Hon), LLD (Hon), EurIng, FIEI, FICE, FIE (Aust), RConsEI, Chartered Engineer
Former Chief Civil Engineer and Chief Operations Engineer, Bord na Móna
Former Director-General, Institution of Engineers of Ireland
Past Chairman, Central Council, Cumann na nInnealtóirí
Past Chairman, Joint Executive, The Institution of Civil Engineers of Ireland and Cumann na nInnealtóirí
Past President, The Institution of Engineers of Ireland
President, The Irish Academy of Engineering

M. Brendan Clancy, BE, FIEI, Chartered Engineer
Former Assistant Chief Executive – Technical, Aer Rianta

W. Gerard Condon, BE, FIEI, FIEE, Chartered Engineer
Former Head of Transmission and Data Networks Department, EIRCOM

William Connellan, BE, FIEI, FIAE, FCILT, EurIng, Chartered Engineer
Chairman of Veolia Environment Companies in Ireland
Former Director General of the Confederation of Irish Industry, and Chairman of the National Roads Authority
Past President of the Institution of Engineers of Ireland and the Irish Academy of Engineering

Ronald C. Cox, MA, MAI, PhD, MICE, FIEI, FIIS, FIAE, Chartered Engineer
Engineering Historian
Director, Centre for Civil Engineering Heritage, Trinity College Dublin
Former Senior Lecturer in Civil Engineering, Trinity College Dublin

John W. de Courcy (*deceased*), ME, FIStructE, FIEI (Hon), Chartered Engineer
Former Associate Professor of Civil Engineering Structures, University College Dublin

James C.I. Dooge, ME, MSc, EurIng, FIEI (Hon), FICE, FASCE, MRIA, Chartered Engineer
Former Professor of Civil Engineering (University College Cork and University College Dublin)
Past President, Institution of Engineers of Ireland

Donal J. Fingleton, BE (Mech and Elec), FIMI, FIEI, Chartered Engineer
Chief Executive, Volkswagen Audi Division, Motor Distributors Ltd, Dublin

Thomas C. Gallagher, BE, MBA, FIEI, FIHEEM, Chartered Engineer
Former Principal Engineering Adviser, Department of Health and Children, Dublin

Michael H. Gould, Engineering Historian
Former Senior Lecturer, Department of Civil Engineering, Queen's University, Belfast

Patrick J. Hennigan, BE, FIEI, Chartered Engineer
Former Deputy Chief Engineer, Dublin County Council

Patrick O. Jennings, BE, FIEI, MCIT, Chartered Engineer
Former Chief Civil Engineer, Córas Iompair Éireann
Past President of the Institution of Engineers of Ireland

William James McCoubrey, FICE, FIHT, FIEI, FIAE, Chartered Engineer
Former Chief Executive, Roads Service, Northern Ireland

Joseph A.V. McEvoy, BE (Mech and Elec), FIEI, FIEE, FIAE, Chartered Engineer.
Former Managing Director, ASEA Electric (Ireland) Ltd

G. Declan McIlraith, BA, BAI, MSc, FIEI, FICE, Chartered Engineer
Former Engineering Inspector (Roads), Department of the Environment

John J. McKeown, BSc (Hons), Dip P.M., EurIng, MIEI, MICE, Chartered Engineer
Regional Manager, Waterways Ireland, Dublin.

M. Finbar McSweeney, MIEI, Chartered Engineer
Former Executive Director, Arup Consulting Engineers

Gordon S. Millington, OBE, DEng. BSc. FIAE, FICE, FIEI, FIStructE, Hon. FICE, Chartered Engineer
Former Senior Partner, Kirk McClure Morton, Belfast, Consulting Engineers
Past President of the Institution of Engineers of Ireland

John S. Moore, B.Sc., M.Sc., C. Eng., M.I.Mech.E, Chartered Engineer
Former Keeper of the Department of Transport, Ulster Folk and Transport Museum, Cultra, County Down

John J. Moriarty, BE, MA, MIEI, Chartered Engineer
Former Director of the Computer Laboratory, Trinity College Dublin and previously of IBM Ireland Ltd

Sean Mulcahy, BE, FIEI, MIEE, FCIBS, MConsEI, Chartered Engineer
Past President, Association of Consulting Engineers of Ireland

Kevin J. O'Connell, BE, BSc, FIEI, FIEE, Chartered Engineer
Former Director of Engineering, RTÉ

Kevin C. O'Donnell, BE, FIEI, MIWEM, FIAE, Chartered Engineer
Former Chief Engineer, Dublin Corporation

Peter J. O'Keeffe, BE, FIEI, MIHE, FIAE, Chartered Engineer
Former Head of Roads Division, An Foras Forbartha
Past President, Institution of Engineers of Ireland

Trevor L.L. Orr, BA, BAI, MSc, PhD, FIEI, MICE, EurIng, Chartered Engineer
Senior Lecturer in Civil Engineering, Trinity College, Dublin

Pierce T. Pigott, BE, MSc, EurIng, FIEI, AMASCE, FIAE, Chartered Engineer
Former Director of Engineering, Office of Public Works
Past President, Institution of Engineers of Ireland

Colin Rynne, BA, PhD
College Lecturer, Department of Archaeology, University College Cork

Michael J. Shiel, BE, BSc, FIEE, MIEI, Chartered Engineer
Former Head of Sites Department and Director, Commercial, Electricity Supply Board, Dublin

Brian D. Torpey, BE, FIEI, FIStruct.E, FIAE, Chartered Engineer
Former Chief Engineer, Dublin Port Company.

PREFACE

The Irish Academy of Engineering was founded in 1997 as a learned society of the engineering profession with the objective of advancing the science and practice of engineering in Ireland as an essential element in national development and the enhancement of living standards. Amongst the objectives of the Academy are to stimulate interest in the preservation and presentation of Ireland's engineering heritage, and to identify and highlight outstanding Irish engineering achievements.

To this end, it was felt that the story of the engineering of the island should be chronicled in book form. In 2000, a steering committee was set up to guide the project through its initial stages, during which a number of senior members of the Irish engineering profession were invited to contribute articles on the history, development and achievements in their specific areas of engineering endeavour.

Engineering Ireland aims to reflect the unified nature of the engineering profession and the combined contributions of military, civil, mechanical, electrical, and other branches of the profession, to the successful completion of projects throughout the island of Ireland.

Part 1 provides an overview of the history of engineering in Ireland, how an engineering profession evolved, the education and training of engineers, and the establishment and growth of Irish engineering institutions, notably the Institution of Engineers of Ireland (now Engineers Ireland).

In succeeding chapters, the historical development of selected areas of engineering application is presented in a non-technical manner and in the absence of mathematical formulae. It would not be possible in a single volume to cover every area adequately, but it is hoped that readers will gain sufficient insight into the activities of the engineering profession to appreciate the significant and invaluable contribution made by Irish engineers over many decades to the quality and advancement of Irish life.

The members of the steering committee were James Dooge, Finbar Callanan, Pierce Pigott, Ronald Cox, Robert Cuffe, John (Sean) de Courcy, and Michael O'Donnell. Sadly, the last three named passed away before seeing the fruits of their efforts. As Editor and Director of the project, I would like to thank all the members of the steering committee for their wise counsel, the President and members of the Council of the Irish Academy of Engineering for their unqualified support for the project, and last, but by no means least, the many contributors to this volume.

Finally, the Academy acknowledges with gratitude the generous financial support of our sponsors, Irish Rail, Siemens, Dublin Port, Sisks, and Cement Roadstone Holdings. A publication grant from the Heritage Council is also acknowledged with thanks.

Ronald C. Cox, Dublin, 2006

ACKNOWLEDGEMENTS

The Editor and the Irish Academy of Engineering wish to acknowledge the valuable contribution of the late Professor John de Courcy to the recording of engineering history in Ireland. In particular, the introduction to this volume drew extensively on his Dr T.A. McLaughlin Memorial Lecture entitled 'A History of Engineering in Ireland', which was subsequently published in The Engineers Journal, Vol.36, Nos.9/10, September/October, 1985.

The contributions of the late Patrick Raftery, President of the Institution of Civil Engineers of Ireland (ICEI) 1967-68, and others who wrote varying accounts of the historical development of the professional body in the Transactions and Journal, formed a significant source of information for the section on the Irish Chartered Engineering Institution.

The brief history of Cumann na nInnealtóirí (CnaI), compiled in 1985 by tAmhlaoibh O h-Aonghusa (Chairman of Central Council of CnaI, 1966-67), which built on a series of earlier articles in The Engineers Journal by Reggie Jackson, proved to be a vital component of the chronicled history.

The tradition of the annual Presidential Address, begun as far back as 1856, has continued up to the present day. The printed addresses, taken together, form a comprehensive corpus of information concerning the institution's activities and achievements.

The assistance of the following is gratefully acknowledged:

John Callanan and the staff of Engineers Ireland

The staff of Trinity College Library

The staff of the National Library of Ireland

The staff of the Royal Irish Academy

David Griffin and the staff of the Irish Architectural Archive

School of Engineering, Trinity College, Dublin Archives

University College Dublin Archives

The Librarian and Archivist of the Irish Railway Record Society

The Librarian, Archivist and staff of the Institution of Civil Engineers

The Heritage Unit of the Office of Public Works

The Department of Civil, Structural & Environmental Engineering at Trinity College Dublin (for providing the Editor with the facilities necessary to enable the compilation of this history).

Finally, the contributing authors gratefully acknowledge the support and advice of many colleagues in the engineering profession throughout Ireland.

The Irish Academy of Engineering acknowledges with gratitude the generous financial support of our sponsors towards the production costs of this publication.

PICTURE CREDITS

Page number(s) in brackets follow acknowledged source of illustrations.

Department of the Environment, Heritage and Local Government (4, 19, 20, 23, 173, 175); Commissioners of Irish Lights (12, 156); Marathon Oil (14); Roughan & O'Donovan / Narrowcast (15); Institution of Civil Engineers (25, 26); Rupert Fuller (30); École Nationale des Ponts et Chaussées, France (38); Trinity College Dublin Library (39); Brendan Dempsey, Trinity College Dublin (42); Masonic Lodges 212 and 384, Dundalk (42); Larmour, J (1912) *Collected Works of James Thomson* (44); Engineers Ireland (48, 56, 72, 78, 80, 106, 277, 297, 330, 333); Peter Barrow, European Photo Services (54); *Engineers Journal* (59, 66, 67, 68, 84, 189, 197, 223, 278, 282, 316, 317, 318); Royal Irish Academy (65); School of Engineering, TCD (73, 254); University of Limerick (75); Peter O'Keeffe (93, 95); Michael Gould (94, 171); Dún Laoghaire-Rathdown County Council (97); UK Motorway Archive Trust (100); Ruth Delany (103); Fred Hamond (109); Fingal County Council (115); Colin Boocock (118); Irish Railway Record Society/David Murray Collection (119, 123, 124); Dublin City Council (139, 195, 205, 209, 217, 222); *The Engineer* (145); Dublin Port Co.(148, 150); Stena Line (149); John Eagles Photography (157); Short Bros (161, 162); Irish Architectural Archive (163); Alain Demonty (166); Old Drogheda Society (170); Translink (183); Arup Consulting Engineers (184); Doran Consulting (187); Carl Brangan (194); Norbert Tempel (213); Clair Sweeney (1991) *The Rivers of Dublin* (216); Brian Torpey (221); © BSNews (229, 231); Royal Victoria Hospital Archives, Belfast (234, 235); Siemens (237, 316); Commissioners of Public Works (242, 244); Colin Rynne (250, 251); ESB Archives (253, 259, 260, 267); Airtricity (264); Barnard, A (1887) *The Whiskey Distilleries of the United Kingdom* (272); © National Museums and Galleries of Northern Ireland, Ulster Folk & Transport Museum (287, 288); Esler Crawford Photography (294); Finbar Callanan (299); Bord na Mona Archives (301, 303, 306); Philip Nelson (300); RIAC Archives (309, 311, 312); Siemens (316); John Byrne (320); Kevin O'Connell (322); John Moriarty (329, 332).

All other photographs are the copyright of the Editor.

Every reasonable effort has been made to contact the copyright holders of photographs reproduced in this book. Should any involuntary infringement of copyright have occurred, sincere apologies are offered and the owners of such copyright are requested to contact the Editor.

Units of Measurement

Imperial units have been used in relation to all engineering works completed prior to 1970, at which time the Irish construction industry adopted the metric system of units. Metric units have been used in relation to projects completed after that date.

The following approximate conversion factors may be used:

Length

1 inch = 25.4mm

1 foot = 0.3048m

1 yard = 0.9144m

1 mile = 1.609km

Area

1 square inch = 645.2mm^2

1 square foot = 0.0929m^2

1 acre = 0.4047 hectare

1 square mile = 259 hectares

Volume

1 gallon = 4.546 litres

1 million gallons = 4546 cubic metres

1 cubic yard = 0.7646 cubic metre

Mass

1 pound = 0.4536kg

1 Imperial ton = 1.016 tonnes

Power

1 horse power (h.p.) = 0.7457 kilowatt

Pressure

1 pound force per square inch = 0.06895 bar

Part I

Engineering Ireland

1

INTRODUCTION

John (Sean) de Courcy & Ronald Cox

FROM EARLIEST TIMES, humankind has recognised the need for shelter, nourishment, transport, communication, light, and warmth. Later, it was found valuable to organise work and, regrettably, found necessary to wage defensive or aggressive war. In all of these pursuits, men and women have exercised their God-given ingenuity, and from the beginning have practised the various elements that one day would collectively be called engineering. It mattered not that the word 'engineering', or even the word from which it would eventually be derived, had not yet crossed the lips of our forebears — they knew the power of horses long before they knew of horsepower; their ability to plough preceded their study of the shear characteristics of soils; and indeed the gravity of the apple was appreciated many scores of centuries before Newton imprudently but so momentously rested in his orchard. But the origins, the concepts were there; the roots of the tree of engineering had been established.

Engineering Ireland tells the story of the development of engineering within Ireland, from the earliest attempts at construction to the technological achievements of the nineteenth and twentieth centuries.

Engineering in Remote Antiquity: 7000 BC to 600 BC

Whilst our archaeology cannot quite match the scale and splendour of the pyramids at Gîza, the builders of this period did leave us with some outstanding structures, for example the tumuli of Newgrange, Knowth and Dowth in County Meath. The tumulus at Newgrange was built in about 3000 BC and, as an organised engineering project of nearly 5,000 years ago, it was formidable. The mound, which is about 40 feet high, contains perhaps 33,000 cubic yards of transported material, mostly loose stone. The surface layer would appear to have been in part white quartz, possibly conveyed 50 miles from County Wicklow. The passage leading to the sepulchral chamber is roofed with stone slabs up to 10 foot in length and each weighing about 3½ tons. It is thought that these stones of Silurian grit or slate were quarried in Slane or near the site of old Mellifont Abbey, both between three and four miles distant. The main chamber is basically circular in plan with a diameter of approximately 20 feet and has a roughly hemispherical roof that reaches a height of 20 feet

Newgrange, County Meath, dating from c. *3000* BC.

over floor level. The roof, which is formed by progressively corbelled flat slabs of stone, supports the weight of about 20 foot depth mound of material covering the chamber. The organisation of the workforce employed on this project, the acquisition and placing of the mounded material, the problem of quarrying and transporting the passage slabs, and the conception and construction of the chamber roof would still today be seen as a significant engineering exercise. Other labour-intensive projects were completed throughout this period, and, towards its end, these included earth-works of the form generally described as ring forts. When one recognises that the ramparts of some of these enclosures were perhaps up to 10 feet in height, one must again be impressed at the organised effort of the early 'engineers' using primitive tools.

Engineering in Antiquity: 600 BC to AD 1170

The Celts arrived in Ireland in about 600 BC and were masters of the spoked and iron-tyred wheel, and the iron-tipped ploughshare. Their understanding of earthworks was evident in their mining and shaft-sinking technology, and in their use of timber-reinforced earth. It seems clear that this skill was linked to the increased use at around that time of the *crannóg* or lake dwelling site as a building form in which related techniques were used — a form that would continue to be built for perhaps 2,000 years.

Elsewhere in the western world, the concept of engineering as a broad unified discipline was already becoming clearer. Archimedes' proud statement of the engineer's capacity — 'give me a place to stand and I will move the world'

— was supported by his skill in mathematics, physics, astronomy and geometry, mechanics, hydrostatics, and machine design. He may be seen as the prototype engineer, basing his practice not only on craft which was, and still remains, essential, but also on mathematical and scientific theory and laws.

In Vitruvius we meet the textbook writer, the recorder of established practice, who treats in a single book of ten parts such diverse matters as the design of foundations, the properties of materials, the function, proportion and strength of buildings, the location, storage and distribution of water, surveying, mechanics, the manufacture of dyes and the design of machines for peace and war. Here again, 50 years before the time of Christ, is a recognition of the unified discipline and vocation of engineering.

During much of this period, the rules for living in Ireland were rooted in the Code of Brehon Law, and here engineering received its due attention. The master builder was skilled in stone and timber, and also constructed mills, sea ships, barques, and bridges. As there is no clear evidence to show that the Irish built stone bridges before the Anglo-Norman invasion, bridges at that time in Ireland were probably very simple wooden structures,. The water mill was well known in Ireland by the sixth century and skills in the forging of iron and mining techniques continued to develop.

Christian missionaries arrived in Ireland in the fifth century, bringing with them new skills and practices from the European mainland. Chief amongst these was a change to stone building, displayed, for example, in the round towers. These were built in masonry, up to 125 feet high, using lime-mortar, a material which, it is suggested, was probably unknown in Ireland before the seventh century. Throughout the country, kilns were built to burn the limestone to produce the lime required.

A new use for earthwork made its appearance in Ireland in the ninth century with the arrival of the Norse settlers. Seafarers, and international traders, the Vikings recognised the need for formal havens for their fleets. In establishing settlements in Dublin and Waterford, they included tidal protection for their waterside settlements, in the form of earth banks and stone walls.

From the Normans to the Restoration: 1170 to 1660

From 1170 to 1660, Irish engineering changed very little, except for the organisational disciplines brought in by the Anglo-Normans. There was a surge of massive building in stone, both ecclesiastical and secular — for example, the great castles of Trim, Carrickfergus and Limerick, and a profusion of monasteries and abbeys. The first stone bridges were built. Whilst the design of major bridges in timber was to continue right through to the nineteenth century, important masonry arch bridges were erected in the thirteenth and fourteenth centuries, as for instance, at Leighlin and Kilcullen, at Ballisodare and at Ballybough in Dublin.

There were, however, some new departures. Amongst these, one reflecting the twelfth-century development of Irish shipping, and in particular the importance of Waterford as the premier Irish port in early Norman times, saw the establishment on Hook Head of the first formal lighthouse on the Irish coast. This was erected probably about 1180 and placed in the charge of the Augustinians. Subsequently rebuilt in the seventeenth century, the Hook light is now the longest in continuous use of all lighthouse sites on the coastline of Britain and Ireland.

Another early initiative was the concept of a community water supply. The planning and provision of a supply for Dublin, in about 1250, used water from the River Dodder at Templeogue and conveyed it by open channel to a basin near St James' Street. The distribution to the citizenry was generally by standpipe, although certain influential persons received individual connections.

A later broader development was in surveying and mapping. Until the sixteenth century, the shape of Ireland presented in atlases was still based on the notional description that had been given by Ptolemy in the second century. Giraldus Cambrensis would seem to have used a version of this map in his twelfth-century writings, and the map of Ireland in Munster's mid-sixteenth-century geography retains the same rather amoebic outline. However, in the days of Elizabeth I's campaigns, and following Cromwell's adventure into Ireland, more accurate details were needed, not only of the coasts, but also of inland features. The resultant series of maps, starting with those of John Speed in 1610 and continuing through the Down Survey directed by William Petty in Munster, Ulster and Leinster (completed 1656), established for the first time what were substantially the correct shape and proportions of the whole island of Ireland.

Restoration to the Union: 1660 to 1800

Developments in this period from Ormonde to Grattan suggest that it may be called the first modern phase of 'Irish' engineering. Ireland and Britain were drawing closer together on engineering matters, with common interests. Ideas, schemes and inventions initiated in one country were quickly being recommended for adoption in the other. Stipendiary practitioners and 'gifted amateurs' would soon be moving in increasing numbers back and forth across the Irish sea.

For the first time, one begins to distinguish between the Irish engineer and the Irish architect. William Robinson, architect of the Royal Hospital at Kilmainham (1680), was described as 'not simply an architect', and again as a professional engineer holding a military appointment, as Surveyor General. His successor, Colonel Thomas Burgh, is regarded as the first indisputable and unmistakable Irish architect. Burgh designed the library at Trinity College (1712) and Dr Steevens' Hospital (1721). But we also know that he was a consultant to Dublin on its water supply and that he made recommendations to Dublin for the improvement of its port. This then was the architect as engineer. Perhaps from here on we may see the engineer's role in building as one of strength, stability, and services. In industrial and mechanical work, and in such structures as bridges, harbours, and fortifications, the engineer retained the role of arbiter of form as well as function.

An Irish industry that was to die out in the eighteenth century was the smelting of iron. It is reckoned that there were about 170 iron works active in Ireland between 1600 and 1800, the most long-lived being a works at Enniscorthy in County Wexford which operated for 232 years from 1560 to 1792. These iron works smelted with charcoal, at a price so competitive with British charcoal that some English and Welsh iron-masters sent their ore to Ireland for smelting and conversion to pig iron, or bar iron, for sale in Britain. However, the discovery of coke smelting, by Abraham Darby of Coalbrookdale in about 1710, and the development of this much cheaper process during the eighteenth century, effectively eliminated charcoal smelting and the industry based on it, in Ireland and elsewhere.

Irish engineering in the eighteenth century was very closely linked to new or improved communication and transport systems. The advantages to be gained from the transport of goods and passengers by canal and river navigation led to an era of inland navigation improvement and construction. The Newry Canal, constructed between 1731 and 1734 to link Lough Neagh with Newry, was the first summit-level navigation of the canal era in either Britain or Ireland. The first large-scale project in Ireland, the Grand Canal system, was commenced in 1755 to link Dublin with the Shannon and the Barrow. The planning and construction of many other lines of inland navigation throughout Ireland followed the Grand Canal system.

Royal Canal at Richmond Harbour.

Improvements to access for shipping to the port of Dublin were begun, one square mile of land being reclaimed on the north shore of the River Liffey, whilst on the south bank construction of the Great South Wall with timber piling was begun in about 1715 and culminated in a stone breakwater and causeway 3 miles long, terminating at Poolbeg lighthouse, built in 1767. This seawall is considered to be one of the major harbour-improvement achievements in Europe in the eighteenth century.

On the roads of Ireland, the eighteenth century saw a re-introduction of wheeled traffic for travel throughout the country rather than merely within towns or through private lands. The rapid development of Ireland's extensive road network resulted from the sequence of the Grand Jury activity beginning in 1634; the Turnpike Trusts, beginning with tolls on the roads from Dublin to Kilcullen and to Navan in 1729; the stage-coach experiments from 1740 onwards; and the mail-coach system from 1789. Arthur Young was to comment in 1780, 'For a country so very far behind us as Ireland, to have got so much the start of us in the article of roads is a spectacle that cannot fail to strike the English traveller exceedingly.'

From the Union to Independence: 1800 to 1920

As a result of the invention by Thomas Newcomen in 1705 of the atmospheric engine, and the patent of James Watt in 1769 for 'a new method of lessening the consumption of steam and fuel in fire engines', the first Industrial Revolution laid the foundations for a bewildering diversification of activity in Irish engineering in the following century. The nineteenth century, the period of the main Industrial Revolution, was also a century of wars and great famines, as well as the making of great fortunes. In Ireland, the use of wind power did not expand; water power held its ground, and, in the latter years, steam power expanded enormously. In 1860, Charles Hodgson established a peat-briquette factory between Monasterevan and Portarlington. Coal gas, first used to light a room in 1760, was used in public and domestic lighting systems. The first gas engines appeared in 1859, followed in 1890 by paraffin-oil engines.

In 1844, Sir Robert Kane (1809–1890), in his monumental study on *The Industrial Resources of Ireland*, presented a strong case for the further utilisation of water power and, in particular, drew attention to the '33,950 horsepower in continuous action day and night throughout the year' in the 100-foot fall of the Shannon between Killaloe and Limerick, the site where the power station of the Shannon Scheme was to be completed in 1929.

Towards the end of the century, Charles Parsons (1854–1931) of Birr Castle invented and developed the steam turbine and later the world's first marine steam turbine. These developments led to the construction of turbo-alternators for the production of electricity on a large scale.

A symbol of the Industrial Revolution in Ireland was perhaps the flax and linen industry in the north of the country. Here the change from hand spinning to power spinning, the use of water power, then steam, was accompanied, not surprisingly, by the decline of small family firms and the rise of the factory system. Engineering input included power systems, Jacquard looms, and the design and manufacture of textile machinery in Belfast, an initiative that found a rich market abroad as well as at home, from around 1850 onwards.

Clearly linked with the industrial activity of the time were the advances in steel making introduced by Bessemer, Siemens, and Thomas between 1856 and 1878. But while steel is the metal that has dominated our engineering thinking since then, mention must be made of the mid-century work of Richard Turner (1798–1881), the Dublin iron-founder and engineer, whose space structures in wrought and cast iron, especially for the glasshouses in the botanical gardens of London, Dublin and Belfast, still receive international acclaim. Also based in Dublin, Robert Mallet (1810–1881) was 'a mechanical engineer in the widest sense and a metallurgist in the narrower sense . . . with a strong bias towards manufacturing'. His pioneering work on the electro-chemistry of corrosion, his anticipation of the modern petrochemical technique of explosive 'fracturing', and his patented work on buckled wrought-iron plates are but a few of his engineering achievements.

In the 1870s, another eminent Victorian, Bindon Blood Stoney (1828–1909), Chief Engineer to the Dublin Port and Docks Board, and considered to be the father of Irish concrete, used pre-cast concrete blocks, each weighing upwards of 350 tons, in the construction of deepwater quay walls. His comprehensive textbook of 1873 on *The Theory of Strains in Girders and Similar Structures*, resulting from his work on the Boyne Viaduct and other structures, was widely consulted. Reinforced concrete was not used in its modern form in Ireland until the 1890s. The Mizen Head fog station pre-cast concrete arch footbridge of 1909 is an early example of international heritage importance.

In maritime structures, the important work of John Rennie (1761–1821) and his son, Sir John Rennie (1794–1874), in designing the Royal refuge harbours at Howth, Kingstown (Dún Laoghaire) and Donaghadee set the standard for many other harbours. Between them, George Halpin (c.1775–1854) and his son of the same name designed and supervised the building of 55 lighthouses, including such lights as those on the Tuskar Rock, on Great Skellig, and the first tower on the Fastnet Rock. The classic work of Francis Giles (1787–1847) and Halpin (Snr) on the North Bull Wall breakwater at Dublin in 1825, which led to the eventual deepening of the approach channel to Dublin port, was of major engineering importance.

Turning to nineteenth-century transport, and beginning with the canals so vigorously being built by 1800, one senses that early in the century, at the same time as the canal trade was expanding, the agencies that would eventually destroy them as commercial enterprises were already waiting in the wings. In 1825, the year of the Stockton–Darlington railway, steamboats were used in the Irish canal system for the first time. In 1837, the Grand Canal transported 101,000 passengers on its packet boats, and carried 216,000 tons of goods.

A symbol of the vigour and unity of nineteenth-century engineering in Ireland is to be seen in the building of the railways. The first public passenger railway in Ireland (the Dublin & Kingstown) was opened on 17 December 1834, and in 1844 carried 1,962,000 passengers on its service of over 80 trains per day. Railway construction presented a number of engineering challenges, such as the crossing of the River Boyne near Drogheda, where wrought-iron latticed girders were used, and the extensive masonry of the Craigmore arch viaduct — both on the Dublin–Belfast line — the Kells mountain traverse near Cahirciveen, and the Cork approach tunnels.

Whilst much orthodox mechanical engineering on rolling stock was carried out in Ireland, principally at the Inchicore and Dundalk engine works, locomotive engineers, such as Alexander McDonnell (1829–1904) were highly regarded as locomotive designers. The extension from Kingstown (Dún Laoghaire) to Dalkey operated between 1844 and 1854 on the atmospheric or vacuum principle.

Ireland's contributions to basic developments in electricity and communications included Nicholas Callan's invention of the induction coil and George Francis Fitzgerald's development of the electro-magnetic theory of radiation. Ireland also welcomed Guglielmo Marconi to Ireland in 1907 to establish his transatlantic wireless station just south of Clifden in County Galway.

The only practical applications of electricity in Ireland prior to 1880 were in communication by telegraph, by electric bell, and by telephone. The last named came in about 1877, the year when William Henry Preece used Alexander Graham Bell's telephone to speak from Holyhead to Dublin, and Captain Purcell of the Dublin Fire Brigade is said to have installed what was possibly Ireland's first private telephone. In 1857, the first attempt was made to lay a telegraph cable across the Atlantic to North America.

From 1880, electrical engineering in Ireland developed rapidly. In 1883, a tramway from Portrush to the Giant's Causeway in County Antrim became the first in the world to be run on electricity, obtained from a hydroelectric power station on the River Bush near Bushmills. By 1895, tramways were operating in Dublin and, in 1896, the Dublin–Belfast railway was pioneering electric lighting in its trains, using the motion of the train as a power source. By 1903, the electricity generating station at the Pigeon House in Dublin had taken over from the small experimental plant, which had earlier been established in Fleet Street in the city in 1892, an international prototype for a city supply. In parallel with this initiative, large- and small-scale electricity supply systems were being planned for town supplies in many parts of the country.

In 1809, a Commission, presided over at first by Charles Vallancey, was established 'to enquire into the nature and extent of the several bogs in Ireland and the practicability of draining and cultivating them'. The Commission engaged nine engineers and 40 surveyors for about four years, among them Alexander Nimmo, Richard Griffith, William Bald, David Aher, and Richard Edgeworth, to undertake these pioneering surveys.

Between 1824 and 1846, Ireland was the scene of an 'industrial revolution in map making', with the completion of

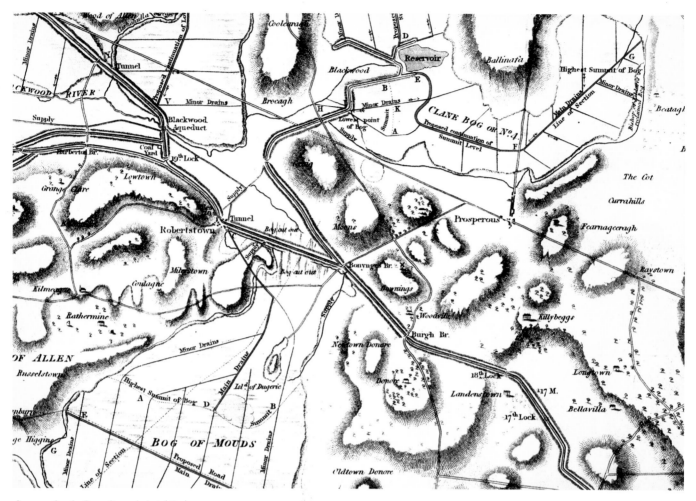

Surveys for the Bogs Commission (1813).

a survey of the whole island to a scale of 6 inches to one mile, the first time in the world that a country had been mapped to such a large scale. The Spring Rice report of 1824, whilst satisfied that earlier bog survey work had established in Ireland a 'school of scientific topography', considered it inexpedient to employ any of 'the respectable civil engineers of Ireland under the authority of the ordnance'. Meanwhile Wellesley, the Lord Lieutenant, insisted, a trifle uncivilly, that Irish engineers could not be employed, holding that 'neither science, nor skill, nor diligence, nor discipline, nor integrity sufficient for such a work can be found in Ireland'. In 1824, a base line was established by military personnel on the east shore of Lough Foyle, and in 1837 the Poolbeg levelling datum was adopted and was to remain in use until a new datum at Malin Head in County Donegal was established in the 1970s.

Land reclamation and arterial drainage were at the time areas of political interest, with the River Shannon obviously a prime topic. In 1821, John Rennie began a commissioned study of the river, and after his death, this work continued through the 1830s under John Fox-Burgoyne, then chairman of the newly founded Board of Works for Ireland (1831) and the founding President of the Society of Civil Engineers (1835), later to become the Institution of Civil Engineers of Ireland (ICEI). Two major Drainage Acts followed, in 1824 and 1863, and their implementation saw 600 square miles of new drained land by 1896. Amongst those engineers who gave much of their lives to this work was Robert Manning, who was to commence his observations on arterial drainage in a paper to the ICEI in 1851, and to follow it in 1889 with his classic paper 'On the flow of water in open channels and pipes'.

During this period, the value of the drained bogs as a source of fuel was also being examined. With hindsight, it seems very fitting that the first paper in Volume 1 of the *Transactions of the Institution of Civil Engineers of Ireland* was Robert Mallet's study, 'On the artificial preparation of turf, independently of season or weather'. The study of peat as a fuel continued right through the period up to the Irish Peat Enquiry of 1917–1920, whose committee, under the chairmanship of Sir John Purser Griffith, included amongst others, Hugh Ryan and Pierce Purcell. The committee's practical promotion of peat fuel was to bear fruit in the latter half of the twentieth century in the shape of Bord na Móna.

During the early years of the nineteenth century, the shipbuilding industry in Cork built and fitted out the first paddle steamer in Ireland (1817). The industry was subsequently dominated by such firms as Harland & Wolff and Workman Clark in Belfast, who between them were to build close on 200,000 tons of new shipping in a single year (1902–1903).

Harry Ferguson (1884–1960) was the first to successfully build and fly a heavier-than-air machine in Ireland (1909), and was later to specialise in farm machinery, notably tractors, in collaboration with Ford. Mention should also be made of Adeney, whose papers on the bacterio-chemical aspects of water pollution were — in collaboration with the work of Letts, of the Queen's University in Belfast, on biology and pollution — to influence so strongly the early twentieth-century classical findings of the British Royal Commission on Sewage Disposal. Nor can one omit reference to a combination of science, structural and mechanical engineering that came together in the construction of the great telescope at Birr Castle in County Offaly, completed by the third Earl of Rosse in 1845.

The nineteenth century saw the introduction of explicit engineering education. Early in the century, engineers in Ireland still acquired their knowledge and skill from a combination of private study, practical work, and the advice of their seniors. Sir John Fox Burgoyne, in his address to the first meeting of the Society of Civil Engineers in Dublin on 6 August 1835, expressed his regret that the profession had been 'at a low ebb in Ireland [with] persons without education or skill [bringing] a certain degree of discredit to the country'.

Perhaps partly as a response, Trinity College Dublin in 1842 established the first chair of civil engineering in Ireland and appointed John Benjamin Macneill, probably the leading structural engineer in the country at the time, as the first holder of the Chair. Shortly afterwards, in 1850, schools were established by the Queen's University of Ireland in its colleges at Belfast, Cork and Galway. Later again, from 1882, the Royal University of

Reflecting Telescope at Birr Castle, County Offaly.

Ireland constituted an examining authority in engineering with some teaching functions and, towards the end of the period, an engineering school was established at University College Dublin (1908).

The New State: 1920 to 1985

Following the establishment in 1920 of the Irish Free State and Northern Ireland, the engineering of the two jurisdictions tended to develop along separate lines.

Developments in what became the Republic of Ireland can be considered under three headings: energy, infrastructure and industry. If these are taken in parallel with protected self-dependence, foreign investment and free trade, it is possible to perceive much of the pattern and impact of engineering in Ireland over that period.

Under the heading of energy, the engineering works of the Electricity Supply Board and Bord na Móna were paramount. The long series of hydroelectric enterprises, from Ardnacrusha (1929) to the pumped-storage scheme at Turlough Hill (1974), the fossil-fuelled electricity generating stations at Ringsend in Dublin, Marina in Cork and at Tarbert and Moneypoint, and the peat-burning stations in the midlands and the west form important examples of the synergy of civil, electrical, mechanical and structural engineering.

In transport infrastructure, the mileage of railway track in use in Ireland, south and north, shrank from 3,170 miles in 1920 to around 1,555 miles by 1985. The inland waterway system no longer had any commercial function, but later government investment in the maintenance and refurbishment of the main lines of canal brought about an awakening of the importance of the waterways for tourism and recreational pursuits. High-quality roads were built, but an urgent need had arisen for a coordinated national programme of road development, and there was some evidence of a resurgence of the eighteenth-century turnpike system in the form of toll roads and bridges. Bridge engineering in Ireland took full advantage of the new techniques available, in particular the use of pre-stressed concrete. During this period, two notable public transport initiatives were made in the Dublin area — the Drumm battery-driven train, which operated from 1932 until replaced by diesel traction in 1949, and the Dublin Area Rapid Transit (DART) system, inaugurated in 1984.

Kish Bank Lighthouse.

The provision of Irish airports began with Baldonnel to the west of Dublin, taken over by the Irish Army Air Corps in 1922, and a number of other fields previously operated by the British Royal Flying Corps. The first commercial airport was at Kildonan near Finglas in 1931. Collinstown, now Dublin Airport, was commenced in 1937 and, in the same year, Rineanna was selected as the location for the future Shannon Airport. Cork followed in 1961, and Knock was completed in 1986. The reclamation, preparation, and development of the Shannon complex on land at the confluence of the River Fergus and Shannon Estuary was a. major engineering achievement, comprising, as it did, a combination of many engineering, industrial and entrepreneurial skills.

Extensive harbour developments were completed at, for example, Cork, Drogheda, Dublin, Galway, Limerick and Rosslare. Examples of large marine engineering projects completed during this period are the No. 2 graving dock in Dublin (1957), the innovative Kish Lighthouse (1965), and the development of extensive dock and harbour facilities at Belfast.

In the realm of electrical and electronic engineering, radio and television services were inaugurated in, respectively, 1926 and 1961. A nationwide network of rural electrification (begun in 1946) was substantially completed by the 1970s. The first digital telephone exchange was opened in 1981 and the last manual exchange closed in 1987. The first fibre-optic cable was laid between Portmarnock and Holyhead in 1985 and, in the same year, a digital microwave link was established between Dublin and Belfast.

The period saw concrete replace stone and, to a significant degree, brick become the predominant Irish building material. Structural steel, in finding valuable new outlets in light long-span roof structures, and timber, especially native Irish timber, faced into a new era of use in structural engineering design.

In the field of public health, the principal works of the period were the provision of piped water supplies and waterborne sewerage systems, with appropriate treatment plants, in most towns and the construction of several regional water supply systems providing piped water to rural dwellers over wide areas. The North and South Dublin Main Drainage schemes were completed, the first discharging into a 1.5km long tunnel to the seabed off the nose of Howth and, in the second instance, involving the construction of a tunnel, formed of pre-cast concrete segments, under the bed level of the Grand Canal.

The development of engineering education, training, and research continued, with the universities being joined by the colleges of technology in Dublin, and the national research bodies, the Institution for Industrial Research and Standards (1946), and the National Institute for Planning and Construction Research (An Foras Forbartha) (1964).

The contribution of Irish engineering to industry during this period included the building and operation of four sugar factories, beginning with Carlow in 1928, and the cement works at Limerick and Drogheda (later replaced by the Platin works). Chemical engineering was making itself felt with the establishment of fertiliser factories at Arklow and Cork, the oil refinery at Whitegate on Cork Harbour (1959) and the alumina processing plant at Aughinish on the Shannon Estuary, brought into service in 1984.

The problems of Ireland's soft and watery places continued to be addressed. On the positive side, extensive arterial drainage projects were undertaken in the catchments of the rivers Brosna, Glyde and Dee, Corrib, Feale, Moy, Inny, Deel, and Boyne. On the negative side, the eutrophication of lake waters caused by the discharge of domestic sewage, or animal wastes, or other waterborne phosphorus from land fertilisation, demanded urgent studies.

Extensive lead, zinc, and silver deposits at Tynagh in County Galway were worked from 1966 to 1980, and extensive deposits of copper were discovered in 1970 near Navan in County Meath, which were to be extracted by Tara Mines. In Cork Harbour, modern steel-rolling mills were established at Haulbowline Island and, for a brief period in the 1960s, the Verolme shipbuilding dockyards produced a number of small bulk carriers.

In the Irish agriculture sector, engineering input included the introduction and rapid development of farm machinery, with the virtual total disappearance of the horse as a means of power. There were significant advances during this period in food processing that have continued to the present day.

The invention of the transistor in 1948 and its miniaturisation in 1959 reached out to enrich the world of engineering, whether it was in analysis, design or production, and led to the wholesale use of computers.

The Last Two Decades: 1985 to 2005

The Republic of Ireland awoke from the economic recession of the 1980s to a 'golden age of infrastructure'. The country was a major beneficiary of aid from the European Union in the form of structural funds, in particular the Regional Development, Social, Guidance and Cohesion Funds.

The timely discovery in 1971 by Marathon Oil of a large natural gas field (the Kinsale Field), 50km off the south coast of Ireland in 90m of water, had opened up considerable opportunities for the use of the gas as a fuel in commercial and domestic applications, for the generation of electricity, and as a feed-stock for an expanding pharmaceutical industry. Following the completion of a terminal in 1978, production of natural gas commenced and pipelines were laid from Cork to Dublin and other large centres of population. In 1995–6, the Kinsale Field's two production platforms accounted for 83 per cent of Ireland's gas requirements, but this had fallen to 18 per cent by 2001. A gas connector was laid across the Irish Sea to connect the Irish gas grid with the UK and European networks, and the shortfall was met by imports piped from Britain. Future indigenous production will come from the Seven Heads Field, a satellite field of Kinsale, and the Corrib Field discovered in 1996, 70km off the Mayo coastline, with reserves of 28 billion cubic metres.

In the 1970s and 1980s, there was considerable expansion of the chemical industry in Ireland, largely as a result of the efforts of the Industrial Development Authority (IDA) in attracting foreign companies to establish plants in the country, especially in the Cork region. By 2000, there were some 220 pharmaceutical and chemical plants operating in the Republic, generating exports to the value of €30 billion.

Growing awareness of the effects of human interaction with the natural environment led to the establishment in the Republic of the Environmental Protection Agency (EPA) to provide a source of information on the quality of the environment and to provide advice and assistance to public authorities. The Environment and Heritage Service performs a similar role in Northern Ireland. The engineering profession continues to face many environmental challenges — in particular, controlling air emissions from transportation, pollution of water sources from agricultural and municipal sources, and improving waste management.

Despite considerable investment in the telecommunications sector in the 1980s, Ireland still lagged behind the rest of Europe, but was soon to catch up with the building of the necessary infrastructure and the introduction of a wide range of telecommunication services, including nationwide mobile telephone networks. Competition resulted in lower charges and more choice and quality. In the mid-1990s, Ireland had the fastest rate of growth in mobile telephony in Europe. The investment paid off as knowledge-based industries located in Ireland, providing top-quality employment for the increasing numbers of graduates in electronic, computer and manufacturing engineering. By 1999, Ireland's tele-services were 100 per cent digital, and broadband was introduced the following year. During the 1990s, computer-related industries provided a firm foundation for an expanding Irish economy and contributed, more than any other sector, to the phenomenal industrial growth that took place and to the substantial foreign trade surplus that was generated.

Kinsale Gas Field.

M1 Motorway crossing of Boyne Valley near Drogheda.

Improvement and expansion of existing road, rail, sea and air transport networks formed an essential part of the development of the infrastructure needed to support the growth in the Irish economy. Major projects, including motorways, tunnels, urban transportation systems, such as light rail, and cargo and passenger-handling facilities at air- and sea-ports, have been made possible by significant levels of state investment, aided by sizable grants under various European Union initiatives. Other major infrastructural improvements have been in the area of public health, in particular in the provision of water supplies, liquid and solid waste disposal, and protection of the environment.

Many of the infrastructural projects in the Republic completed in recent years have formed part of one or other of two national development plans, the first of these being for the period 1994–1999 and the most recent that for the period 2000–2005.

As early as the 1970s, it was recognised that growth in the economy, particularly in technology-based industries, would not be possible without well-educated and highly trained professional engineers and technicians. Following the government Engineering Manpower initiative of 1979, the third-level sector embarked on a significant expansion of teaching, research and training facilities in science, engineering and technology, and the numbers of engineering graduates in all sectors began to rise. This growth has also been reflected in the phenomenal rise in membership of the Institution of Engineers of Ireland and allied professional bodies.

Meanwhile, infrastructural developments in transport, telecommunications and public health in Northern Ireland during this period have followed a similar pattern to those in the Republic. The Industrial Development Board (IDB) was established in 1992 to encourage industrial renewal and development. The decline, and in many cases the demise, of many of the textile, engineering and shipbuilding companies in the northeast of the country during the twentieth century has been largely the result of foreign competition. In both jurisdictions, however, the fostering of direct foreign investment, especially in high-technology industries, became a central perspective, with increasing emphasis on the development of the knowledge economy.

We may sometimes wonder whether we have actually made progress and improved the lot of mankind in moving from one generation to the next. A few facts, however, leave us in no doubt that we have moved significantly in a positive direction, despite some setbacks. In 1900, average life expectancy in the UK was approximately 45 years for men and 49 years for women, whilst by 2002, those figures had increased to 76 and 81 respectively. Similarly in Ireland, this increase in life span has been accompanied by greater expectations in the quality of life to which we aspire and a lower tolerance of human exploitation and unnecessary hardship. Very few of us would willingly exchange living conditions now for those encountered 100, or even 50, years ago.

The contribution of the engineering profession — for example, through the provision of clean water and sanitation — has been an essential and intrinsic element in the development of the world of the present century. The greatest proof of this, and indeed the greatest compliment to the engineering profession, is that so much is taken for granted.

To ensure that life goes on each day, large numbers of engineers and technicians play the role of unsung heroes: keeping our water and wastewater systems functioning properly; collecting our waste and ensuring its proper disposal; ensuring that our transport systems operate satisfactorily; providing the energy to meet working and domestic needs; maintaining and improving communications services, and monitoring, controlling and improving environmental performance.

There has been much talk about sustainable development. Sustainability requires a balance between economic, social, environmental and natural resource factors. The Institution of Engineers of Ireland (in October 2005, the IEI became known as Engineers Ireland) accepts that challenge in its mission statement. This is reinforced by the IEI Code of Ethics, which requires members to 'promote the principles and practices of sustainable development and the needs of present and future generations'.

The engineering profession plays a central role in industrial development, in the provision of infrastructure, in education and in innovation, which brings with it a particular responsibility in meeting the challenges that lie ahead.

As the late Professor Sean de Courcy concluded at the end of his McLaughlin Lecture in 1985,

> It seems clear that, as we and our predecessors have moved through history, particularly through the last 150 years, the increasing diversity of our profession may have been weakening our grasp of its essential unity. It would be a pity if in recognising the unity of nature, our tremendous ally and adversary, we were not to foster, with chivalry, a greater unity of our engineering forces also, the better to combat the might of this noble opponent; and it would be a pity if we did not seek, through an increasing awareness of the unity of our profession, to optimise the advantage that our engineering of today can offer the community in which we live.

It seems that the engineering profession in Ireland heeded the Professor's words and is today flourishing and more than ever directing its efforts to serve the wider community.

2

EVOLUTION OF ENGINEERING

James Dooge

THE ROLE OF THE INDIVIDUAL CRAFTSMAN and engineer and the education and training provided for those who wish to follow a career in engineering and technology have changed greatly throughout history and methods of such training have correspondingly passed through many changes. The history of these changes in Ireland may be judged in the context of similar developments in other countries of Western Europe.

Early Craftsmen in Ireland

The origins of engineering go back to prehistoric times. Thus Lewis Mumford, in his seminal work, *Technics and Civilisation*, published in 1946, wrote that: 'The dream of conquering nature is one of the oldest that has flowed and ebbed in man's mind'. The history of this endeavour has been made up of relatively short periods of intense development interspersed with long periods of slower progress. This long process was divided by the Spanish writer Ortega y Gasset into three periods: (a) the era governed by the technology of chance, (b) the era governed by the technology of the craftsman, and (c) the era governed by the technology of the technician. The chance technological discoveries in the early Stone Age were passed on by the primitive inventor to members of his close family circle. Elements of this learning by close observation of an expert have persisted to the modern age. In the second era, that of the craftsman, the method of training slowly became more organised through formal apprenticeship. In the third era, training and education of technicians and engineers became even more systematic.

Human settlers came to Ireland some time before 7000 BC and lived by hunting, fishing and food-gathering. Initially they used stone axes to make clearings in the forests, which were the base of their activities. It is interesting to note that, according to O'Neill (1984), 'The first factory of any kind in Ireland was at Tievebulliagh, 1, 000 foot up on the mountain overlooking Cushendall in North Antrim, where the hard igneous rock was suitable for the making of stone axes. In the Neolithic and Early Bronze Ages axes found their way to many parts of Britain and Ireland.' In the later Stone Age, buildings were constructed from locally available stone. Later, the arrival of new settlers from

Brittany gave rise to developments in masonry such as the remarkable stone masonry represented by the structures in the Boyne Valley, for example Newgrange (2700 BC). The following two millennia saw the construction of thousands of ring forts. The Celts arrived in Ireland about 400 BC and the importance of water in their cosmology and mythology was paralleled by their activity in man-made fords, *crannóg*s and, later, watermills.

In the case of the ancient large-scale civilisations, the transition from craft to profession began at a much earlier date than in Northern Europe. In Egypt, this change took place from about 3000 BC, in Mesopotamia from about 2000 BC, and in Greece from about 500 BC. Imhotep (*c.* 1700 BC), the designer and builder of the first pyramid, is the first engineer whose name is known to us. But the social conditions in Ireland and in the rest of Northern Europe were very different from those in the ancient urban civilisations of the Mediterranean regions and this was reflected in the slower development of the transition from the various crafts to the profession of engineering. The engineer working in those ancient civilisations was primarily responsible for large-scale projects of irrigation, building, and warfare, and acted as an adviser to the ruler of a highly centralised society. In Ireland, the climate made irrigation unnecessary, and the small-scale structure of the essential rural society made the construction of large buildings and the conduct of large-scale warfare irrelevant. Whilst the road system of ancient Ireland was not as systematic as that of the Roman Empire, it was relatively well developed for the purposes of peace and war.

In the old Mediterranean civilisation, though the superintendent had social status, the actual craftsmen were often chattels or slaves. In both pre-Celtic and Celtic Ireland the gap between the landowners and the craftsmen was much narrower. McNeill (1923) wrote: 'In Irish law the skilled craftsman was a freeman ex officio and this tradition of the law has become enshrined in the language: the ward *saor*, meaning free or a freeman, means also a craftsman'. This feature was paralleled by the high status of women, which also derives from the pre-Celtic society. The importance of craftsmen in these very early times is clearly reflected in the mythology and early folklore that has come down to us. Even though the information on these traditions was not written until the fifth century, nevertheless the importance of craft in the earliest times is clearly evident. The Tuatha De Danann recognised a number of craft gods including Goibniu the smith, Luchte the woodworker, Credne the worker in metals, and Dian Cécht the physician. There are indications that Goibniu was recognised as proficient in more than one craft and was the supreme artificer and that his skills included that of healing. In later times, the name Goibhniu was replaced by Gobán and he was referred to as Gobán Saor (Gobán the artificer) and later as An Gobán Saor. In this later folklore Gobán is largely referred to as the builder notable for his ingenuity and his quick wit. A number of stories relating to the building of monasteries in the Middle Ages refer to the name that was apparently applied in general to master builders.

The Brehon Laws distinguished between the rights of different levels of craftsmen. In the list of professions likely to generate sufficient profit for land purchase, the legal texts include craftsmanship in wood or stone and smithcraft and metalwork, together with learning, poetry and law. Thus somebody recognised as skilled in two or three crafts had more rights than persons skilled in only one craft. A person skilled in four crafts had a still higher social status. The term *ollamh*, used nowadays to denote a professor, could be applied to a master craftsman as well as to a poet or a lawyer and entitled him to the same privileges (but not more). In the seventh century, a district ollamh could command an annual retainer of about 20 cows. This high status was largely given for excellence in stone building and wood carpentering and in the Middle Ages was usually the recognition of special work in relation to a stone church or a wooden oratory.

Gallarus Oratory, County Kerry.

The Medieval Master Craftsmen

A key factor in Northern Europe during the not-so-dark Ages (500–900) was the control of the wooded environment by means of improved methods of working on the part of the woodsmen. Mumford (1946) describes the work of the woodsman in the forests of the temperate zones as being the work of 'the primitive engineer'.

An agricultural revolution started in Northern Europe in the early sixth century through the replacement of the light plough used in Southern Europe by a heavy wheeled plough that could handle heavier soils and that made cross ploughing unnecessary. In addition, the new method of ploughing in long strips facilitated the drainage of fields. Little is known about the organisation of craftsmen or their training in this period. However, there are indications that in the monasteries the monks following a given craft lived together in one house and under one master. This must have facilitated training in their chosen or allotted craft.

A commercial revolution took place in Northern Europe between 900 and 1200. In medieval Ireland, there was a new impetus in regard to roads and bridges (both timber and masonry) due both to the intermittent phases of the extension of Anglo-Norman control and to the general medieval progress. The network consisted of five types as follows:

Main roads (*slighe*) (which could allow two large chariots to pass one another)

Connections between the five main roads (*amhrota*)

Roads capable of accommodating a herd of cattle (*bóthar*)

A rural road serving a farm (*tuaghrata*), and

A track capable of accommodating a pack animal.

A key element in this development process was the increase in the use of water mills and in their efficiency. Contrary to what one might expect, it has been recorded that throughout the Middle Ages, water mills were much more common than churches, and this tendency is well exemplified in the case of Ireland. There were considerable advances in water technology throughout the Middle Ages. There are references in the ancient Irish law tracts to watermills in Ireland in the fifth century, and it is now accepted that both horizontal and vertical water wheels were in use in Ireland early in the seventh century. Up to 800, the use of these water mills was confined mostly to the grinding of grain as in classical times. Early in the ninth century, the use of mills was extended to the preparation of mash for beer and, towards the end of the tenth century, stamp mills were used for producing hemp and for the fulling of cloth. Another industry to

Round Tower, Ardmore, County Waterford.

be affected by milling was the various trades concerning the use of metals. Archaeological evidence suggests that the number of Irish horizontal water mills greatly exceeded that of Britain and Europe.

The expansion in the number of water mills was closely connected to the growth of the monastic system and this must have influenced technical training. A contemporary biographer of St Bernard in the twelfth century gives a graphic description of the multiple use of water power in the Abbey of Clairvaux in the twelfth century. This was not the only engineering interest of monks as is evident from the praise of the Archbishop of Mainz for a group of monks of whom he said: 'I have found men after my own heart ... not only do they give witness of unblemished religion and a holy life, but also they are very active and skilled in building roads, in raising aqueducts, in draining swamps — such as have greatly weakened the monastery in that area — and generally in the mechanic arts.'

Another step along the road to the emergence of engineering as a profession was the remarkable change in scale both in the houses of the nobility and in churches. In Ireland, we can trace the transition from the very small Celtic oratories to small Irish Romanesque churches and thence to larger churches in more ornate European Romanesque style. One particular feature of Irish masonry in the Middle Ages was the round towers. Lime-mortar was used in the construction of the round towers but the date and pathway for the introduction of mortar technology to Ireland is not clear. As a result of this change of scale, the role of the master builder evolved from that of a craftsman to one that had many of the features of the modern engineer. The role of the master mason also expanded because of the replacement of wooden bridges by masonry bridges.

In the ancient world, the professional concerned with large-scale construction was termed 'a superintendent'; in classical Greece and Rome, this was replaced by 'architect'; the term 'engineer' first arose in late medieval and renaissance times. Courteney (1997) tells us that 'medieval architects were designers, builders, geometricians and working craftsmen whose skills embraced those of civil engineers, architectural surveyors, purveyors of materials and inventors of machines and mechanical devices'. Because of the many conflicts of the period, these medieval builders were also concerned with military engineering.

From the eleventh century onwards, the training of craftsmen became the concern of the medieval guilds, but there is little information on the education and training of the master craftsmen. An exception is the case of the master mason, who played a vital role in the building of cathedrals and of castles. This role has been described by Courteney as follows:

> A master mason was a hired salaried professional who headed a hierarchical work force consisting of his foreman, fellow masons, journeymen and apprentices in addition to his chief collaborators, the master carpenter and master smith, and supported by common labourers, diggers and carters. The team thus included skilled professionals often imported from elsewhere in addition to local labourers who might be hired on the spot. As various building accounts reveal, master builders received high wages and belonged socially to a superior artisan class.

The team of masons operating under a master mason included hewers, setters, wallers, paviours, rough masons and free masons. Unlike most other medieval craftsmen, masons did not have a fixed residence in a town or city but moved around from project to project.

Renaissance and Military Engineers

Though the tendency is to view the Renaissance as a complete break with the Middle Ages, engineering practice in that period was firmly founded on modifications of medieval practice. The two principal new directions were an increase in the scale of the works undertaken and a change in attitude on behalf of practitioners from the anonymity of the master craftsman in the Middle Ages to the self-assertion of the engineer-architects of the Renaissance. The latter group had not yet divided into separate professional specialisations and many of the names known to us from the Italian Renaissance were at various stages in their careers active in architecture, military engineering and civil engineering. For example, Andrea Palladio (1508–1580) is remembered as one of the most influential architects of the sixteenth century, but he was also the first person to design really efficient roof trusses and to avoid the redundant members, which were a feature of medieval roof trusses, but which added nothing to their strength. He also improved greatly the design of wooden bridge trusses.

The aforementioned characteristics are reflected in the careers of some of the leading figures of the Renaissance period. Most of them were apprenticed to craftsmen and later practised as engineer-architects as well as artists. Filippo Brunelleschi (1379–1446) is best remembered for his innovative design of the dome of Florence Cathedral. He also proved to be an efficient supervisor of construction. He discovered that an inordinate amount of time was being lost through the workmen having to use the series of lofty ladders at mealtime. Brunelleschi remedied this by installing a canteen in the higher levels of the scaffolds. During the seventeen years that it took to complete the dome, he was busy at many other architectural and engineering projects. For example, he received a patent in 1421 for a canal boat equipped with cranes for handling heavy cargoes.

Leon Battista Alberti (1404–1472) was extremely versatile, even by Renaissance standards. He is remembered as a painter, a poet, a philosopher, a musician, an architect and an engineer. That he was genuinely interested in engineering matters is clear from his descriptions of the properties of various types of stone and of wood in relation to construction, which he included in his treatise, *De Re Aedificatoria*, written about 1452. Other topics covered in this treatise on building include foundations, piles, cofferdams, fortifications, bridges, sewers, hydraulics and canal locks.

Donato d'Agnolo Bramante (1444–1514) was responsible for the early design of St Peter's Basilica and for the construction of the four main piers. Apart from other minor architectural work, he devised the screw press for the stamping of coins and independently rediscovered the classical Roman technique of pouring liquid concrete into wooden forms.

Michelangelo Buonarroti (1475–1564) continued the work on St Peter's but was also active at different points in his career on the building of fortifications first in Florence and later in Rome. His 1529 Commission from the Council of War of Florence records his appointment as: 'Governor and procurator general over the construction and fortification of the city walls as well as every other sort of defensive operation and munition of the city of Florence'. Michelangelo also had considerable experience in the building of bridges and the associated cofferdams. All this was in addition to his talents and achievements as a painter, a sculptor and a poet.

The most mechanically minded of the great figures concerned with Renaissance engineering was Leonardo da Vinci (1452–1519). He was apprenticed in Florence to the artist and goldsmith Verrocchio. During his apprenticeship he acquired skills in painting, sculptor, silverwork, bronze casting and ironwork. In 1483, he moved to Milan and there wrote a letter to Lodovico Sforza, the Duke of Milan, seeking employment. In this he claims a wide range of abilities grouped into thirty-six separate paragraphs. Thirty of these related to technical competence and only six to artistic competence. His passionate interest in all things technical, and in mechanical science, was revealed only many years later when his notebooks were published. In 1499, after the end of the Sforza rule in Milan, Leonardo went to Venice, but he soon drifted back to Florence. In 1502, he took up an appointment as a military engineer with Cesare Borgia who referred to him in a 1502 commission as: 'Our very excellent and favourite private architect and engineer General Leonardo da Vinci'. This commission guaranteed Leonardo freedom of movement, exemption from all public taxes, and the right to secure local assistance in surveying and construction. His work at the French Court from 1516 to his death in 1519 varied from work on schemes of canalisation to the design of mechanical lions for royal entertainment.

The changes in society and in the conduct of wars are reflected in the changes in the title of the chief administrator of military engineering in Ireland throughout the centuries. In the thirteenth century, the title had been Keeper of the King's Works of the Castle of Dublin. By 1388, the title had become Clerk of the King's Works with jurisdiction throughout Ireland. In the sixteenth century, the title of the position was Superintendent of the Castles. From 1613 until 1648, this was changed to the title Director General and Overseer of Fortifications and Buildings. During the Commonwealth period, this was changed to Overseer of the Public Works but reverted in 1661 to Engineer-overseer, Surveyor and Director General of the King's Fortifications and Plantations.

The 96 military engineers listed in Loeber's *Biographical Dictionary of Engineers in Ireland 1600–1730* (1981) reflect a variety of backgrounds and countries of origin. The relatively high number of military engineers from France is a

Charles Fort, Kinsale, County Cork.

reflection of the dominance of French expertise in the field at that time. Typical of the military engineers at the beginning of the seventeenth century was Sir Josias Bodley (1550–1617) who was Director General of the Fortifications and Buildings in Ireland from 1607 until 1617. He had studied for a while at Merton College in Oxford but did not take a degree. He chose a military career but little is known about his early life as a soldier until he was sent to participate in the campaign against Hugh O'Neill in 1598. He distinguished himself at the siege of the Spaniards in Kinsale as 'trench master general' and appears to have been in charge of the erection of the siege forts on that occasion. In subsequent years, he was concerned with fortifications at Waterford, Cork and Limerick, and later with the fortifications in Ulster and in Galway. He took a major part with William Parsons in the surveying of the plantation of Ulster in 1609 and again in 1612 and 1616.

Another early military engineer was Roger Boyle (1621–1679), the third son of Richard Boyle, the first Earl of Cork, and a brother of Robert Boyle, the chemist. He is described as a gentleman-architect and engineer. Roger Boyle attended Trinity College Dublin and spent the years 1637–1639 on a grand continental tour during which he took an interest in mathematics, architecture and fortification. In 1641, he returned to Ireland and shortly afterwards took a command in the army because of the outbreak of the rebellion of 1641; he served under Cromwell, but later returned to the Royalist side. Twenty years later, he became Lord President of Munster and was responsible for the fortifications, and in particular the engineering works at Rincurran near Kinsale, which later became known as Charles Fort.

William Molyneux (1656–1696) who jointly with William Robinson held the post of Surveyor General of Fortifications and Buildings, from 1684 to 1696, had a greater interest than his predecessors in the link between theory and practice. During the 1680s, he undertook the study of mathematics and similar problems while living in London. In 1683, Sir William Petty and William Molyneux founded the Dublin Philosophical Society and became respectively the first President and the first Secretary.

Still more typical of the emerging military engineer was Thomas Burgh (1670–1730) who, in 1700, succeeded William Robinson as Surveyor General of Fortifications and Buildings. He was educated at Delaney's School in Dublin and entered Trinity College in 1685. In 1700, he became Surveyor General, and in the following year became Barracks Overseer in Ireland. He was responsible for the supervision of the construction of such notable Dublin landmarks as the first Custom House and Trinity College Library.

The First Civil Engineers

The leading engineers in Britain in the eighteenth century still came from a background of craft training. Thus James Brindley (1716–1772) started life as a millwright before commencing his pioneering work on canal building. John Smeaton (1724–1792) trained as a watchmaker before becoming interested in scientific topics and becoming the prototype of the professional civil engineer. Thomas Telford (1757–1834) was a stonemason before becoming involved in engineering work on canals, road making, bridges, railways, harbour engineering, water supply and many other activities.

The transition to professionalism in civil engineering as distinct from military engineering in the second half of the eighteenth century may best be understood from reading Alec Skempton's life of John Smeaton, published in 1981. Smeaton was interested in mechanical work from an early age. He set up a workshop in London for instrumentation and employed three craftsmen as his assistants. Meanwhile, he became a regular attendee at meetings of the Royal Society and presented six papers to the Society between 1748 and 1752, and in 1753 was made a Fellow. His paper on the subject of his model experiments on water mills and windmills won him the prestigious Copley medal of the Royal Society in 1759. Already he had been recommended in 1756 by the President of the Royal Society as the most suitable person to design the replacement for the Eddystone Lighthouse, which had been destroyed by a storm in December 1755. The success of this work launched him on an engineering career, which encompassed a virtually unbelievable range of projects.

What distinguished Smeaton from his contemporaries was his emphasis on professionalism. In his approach, he combined design principles, professional ethics and organisation of his practice in a manner that was to set the standards for the emerging profession. He prescribed in detail the structure of the site management and the respective duties of the engineer-in-chief and the resident engineer. Smeaton formalised engineering apprenticeship but himself took only one pupil at a time.

Inevitably the emergence in Ireland of civil engineering from the more complex profession of architect-

John Smeaton (1724–1792) (Institution of Civil Engineers)

engineer-builder followed closely on the lines of that in England. The developments in the second half of the eighteenth century in Ireland may be illustrated by noting the careers of two architect-engineers (Richard Castle and David Ducart), one gentleman-engineer (Richard Lovell Edgeworth), one military-engineer (Charles Vallancey) and one civil engineer (William Chapman). All of these engineers worked in Ireland and owed their knowledge of the subject to extensive observation and reading.

Richard Castle (or Cassel) (1695–1751) was born in Germany and had travelled widely in Germany, the Low Countries and France, before coming to England and on to Ireland in 1728. Castle wrote what is probably the first available account of canal engineering in the English language. He was in sole charge of the Newry Canal (the first summit-level canal in these islands) from 1733 to 1736. A few years later, he published an essay on possible approaches to providing a water supply for Dublin. Castle was the architect for Leinster House and the Rotunda in Dublin, for Carton House in County Kildare, and for Powerscourt House in County Wicklow.

Davis Ducart (*c.* 1735–*c.*1785) was apparently from Italy and, like Castle, is better remembered as an architect than as an engineer. He has been described as the last of the Palladians. In regard to engineering, he was associated with the project of the three-mile canal from Drumglass to Coalisland in connection with the Tyrone Collieries, which was notable for the first use in these islands of canal inclines rather than lock gates.

Richard Lovell Edgeworth (1744–1817) was a typical gentleman-engineer. As a youth, he was interested in things mechanical and his intellectual interests were stimulated through his having the freedom of the library of his relative,

Lord Longford, at Pakenham Hall. He was a man of wide interests including the promotion of education in Ireland, encouraging his daughter Maria to write her famous novels, and in many aspects of engineering. These included experiments on transport in regard to the design both of carriages and of roads, the diversion of the River Rhone to a new channel, and methods of telegraph communication.

Charles Vallancey (1725–1812) was educated at Eton and at the Royal Military College. In the 1750s, he started to translate works on military engineering from the French, in order to obtain money to support his family of twelve children. These translations were followed in the 1760s by works on civil engineering, including a substantial treatise on inland navigation, drawing on the work of Guglielmini, Michelini, Castelli and Belidor, with additional material relating to the practice of Dutch and German engineers. He translated from the French a treatise on stone cutting by de la Rue.

William Chapman (1749–1832) worked on a full time basis in Ireland from 1783 until 1794 and was representative of the new breed of civil engineer. He received a liberal education at different public schools, spent three years as master of a merchant vessel trading with the Continent, and developed a keen interest in harbour engineering. At the age of 34, he became an agent for Boulton and Watt in connection with colliery machinery in County Tyrone. He was later employed for two years as an engineer on the Kildare Canal where he introduced the modern masonry skew bridge. From 1789 onwards, he worked on the Grand Canal and reported on other schemes for inland navigation. On the death of his father, he returned to England where he was responsible for a variety of engineering works.

In view of the above transition, it is not surprising to find a variety of educational backgrounds in the case of engineers who were prominent in Ireland in the early nineteenth century and this will be discussed further in 'Engineering Training and Education'.

Thomas Telford (1757–1834).

In contrast to Continental Europe, in Britain, the development of engineering towards the professional status traditionally enjoyed by the Army, the Law and the Church was a matter of sporadic evolution rather than central planning. In the eighteenth century, discussions on science as well as other topics took place in the coffee houses of London, often in the form of informal dining clubs. In 1771, John Smeaton invited seven of his associates in engineering to meet at the King's Head in Holborn to form a dining club for the purposes of discussing questions of engineering interest. Four of these eight founding members were Fellows of the Royal Society. The average age of the original members was just under 50. After Smeaton's death in 1792, the Society lapsed but was revived the following year by John Rennie and Robert Mylne, and was renamed the Smeatonian Society. The Society still exists as a Dining Club.

In late 1817, on the completion of his pupillage, Henry Palmer (1795–1844) proposed the formation of a society of persons studying the profession of a civil engineer. The average age of the founders of this new society was 25, and membership was originally limited to persons between the ages of 20 and 35. The society made little progress in its first two years and failed to expand to include established engineers. In 1820, the officers asked Thomas Telford to take over as President of the Society in order to set the society, now renamed as an institution, on a more solid footing. Telford indicated that he was fully aware of the necessity for such a body but had not been aware of the founding of this institution. He devoted a good deal of time and energy to establishing the institution on a sound footing and, in 1828, the Institution of Civil Engineers, whose membership now exceeded 100, applied for and received a Royal Charter.

From Fortifications to Public Works

The changes in the nature of engineering practice in Ireland continued into the first half of the nineteenth century. Military engineers continued to play a key role in the organisation of engineering works but these works were concerned with the development of infrastructure rather than the protection of the island from foreign invasion.

An interesting early transition between the two periods was the work of the Bogs Commission, which was responsible for detailed surveys from 1807 to 1812. The chairman of the Commission was General Charles Vallancey, then over 80 years of age. Among the engineers who wrote the 25 individual survey reports were Richard Lovell Edgeworth, then in his mid-sixties, previously referred to as a gentleman-engineer of the eighteenth century, and Alexander Nimmo, with his university background, who had joined the Commission in 1811 at the age of 28.

Career military officers continued to play a key role in the organisation of large-scale projects of public importance in Ireland. Prominent among these was John Fox Burgoyne (1782–1871) who was the first President of the Society of Civil Engineers, later to become the Institution of Civil Engineers of Ireland. He had fought in the Peninsular War where he was twice wounded. In 1831, he accepted the chairmanship of the newly established Board of Public Works (Ireland) (1831). His task was to take over a number of public areas of activity previously administered by boards of unpaid commissioners who were not able to discharge efficiently their responsibilities (government loans, inland navigation, roads, public buildings, district asylums, fisheries). Burgoyne was a member of the commission set up to advise on the development of Irish railways. He advocated a public works approach to both the planning of the network and the execution of the works. He was not successful in regard to the latter but his approach was vindicated some 30 years later when the 22 Irish railway companies were exhibiting a range of non-profitability from non-payment on preference stock, to bankruptcy. He returned to service in the Corps of Engineers in 1845, but was recalled to Ireland as chairman of the Famine Relief Commission in 1847.

Thomas Larcom (1801–1879) was also a career officer in the Corps of Engineers. He worked for a while on the Ordnance Survey in England and then was transferred to Dublin to the Ordnance Survey of Ireland and was put in charge of the latter in 1826. He was responsible for initiating the extension of the work of the survey to record natural features, agricultural and industrial practices, antiquities and local customs. Between 1846 and 1858, he was a Commissioner for Public Works and was vice-chairman under Richard Griffith from 1850 to 1853. He had major responsibility for overseeing the 12,000 supervisory staff on the relief schemes in the famine years. In 1851, he had the added responsibility of Census Commissioner. In 1853, he was appointed Under Secretary for Ireland.

William Thomas Mulvany (1806–1885) joined the Ordnance Survey of Ireland under Thomas Larcom in 1826 as an assistant surveyor and, a year later, transferred to a similar position in the Boundary Survey under Richard Griffith. In 1835, he became an assistant engineer on the Shannon Navigation, a civil engineer in 1836, and a district engineer in

1839. He became a protégé of Burgoyne and assisted the latter in drawing up the draft Bill, which became the landmark Arterial Drainage Act of 1842. Mulvany was appointed a member of the Drainage Commission (1842–1845) and was a member of the Commission of Public Works from 1846 to 1853. In 1845, following the first failure of the potato crop, Mulvany drafted a special report urging the streamlining of procedures in the 1842 Act. This resulted in the Summary Proceedings Act of 1846. Under the latter legislation, the number of new applications for schemes increased to 81 in 1846, compared to six in 1845. The number of new works com-

Shannon Harbour, terminus of the Grand Canal.

menced increased from four in 1845 to 45 in 1846, and to 47 in 1847. When the crisis was over, the Irish landlords attacked Mulvany's administration of these works through a House of Lords Committee of Inquiry. Mulvany was obliged to resign on pension at 46 years of age. In 1855, he went to the Ruhr, then an agricultural region, to develop deep-mining activities on behalf of Irish investors. He is remembered today as one of the leading figures in the development of the Ruhr economy.

In the last quarter of the eighteenth century and the first quarter of the nineteenth century, most native-born engineers served only as assistant surveyors and as assistant engineers or as contractors on schemes designed by consulting engineers from Britain. One notable exception was John Killaly (1766–1832) who completed both the Grand and Royal Canals to the River Shannon and became in time engineer to the Directors General of Inland Navigation. The first substantial contracting firm run by Irish-born engineers was founded by three engineers who link the canal era to the era of public works: David Henry, John McMahon and Bernard Mullins. In 1802, Henry and Mullins successfully bid for the contract to complete the final section of the Grand Canal. In 1806, Henry, Mullins and McMahon received a contract to restore and extend the Kildare Canal built by William Chapman in 1787–1789. Bernard Mullins set out his views on inland navigation in a brief study, which was published in 1832. He worked under Chapman on the Kildare Canal and under Evans on the Royal Canal. David Henry was an engineer-architect, Bernard Mullins a canal engineer, and John McMahon a waterways and bridge engineer. In 1824, they commenced the extension of the Grand Canal to Ballinasloe and, in 1827, the Barrow Aqueduct at Monasterevan. Mullins and McMahon continued in partnership until 1842 when McMahon joined the newly established Arterial Drainage Section of the OPW set up by William Mulvany. He was one of the six engineers recruited by Mulvany at the start of the implementation of the 1842 Arterial Drainage Act.

From Canals to Railways

During the first half of the nineteenth century, a centrally planned network providing for a wider system of communication eventually replaced the somewhat haphazard development of local roads under the Grand Jury system, but the transport of bulk goods by road was still uneconomic. The canal mania of the late eighteenth century, based on private initiative, had provided a viable alternative, and construction of extensions to the network continued into the nineteenth century, but canal transport was in turn to be replaced by the construction of a co-ordinated railway network.

The versatility of the engineers of the first quarter of the nineteenth century may be exemplified by the work in Ireland of the Scottish civil engineer Alexander Nimmo (1783–1832). He commenced his engineering career under Telford for the Commission on Highland Roads, mapping the boundaries between counties. From 1811 to 1813, he worked in Ireland for the Bogs Commission as one of the nine engineers responsible for individual regions. He reported on the bogs of Kerry and Cork and Connemara. In 1814, he commenced work on the planning of a pier and harbour at Dunmore East in County Waterford. In 1815, he made a visit to engineering works in France, Belgium, Holland and Germany, where he took a particular interest in the French system of organising engineering education and engineering public works, and on his return was engaged in public works, such as roads, bridges and piers. Between 1821 and 1831, he supervised many schemes for the Congested Districts Board, including the development of Roundstone village and harbour in County Galway. In 1825, he proposed a railway between Limerick and Waterford, and in 1831, planned the rail link between Dublin and Kingstown, later completed by Charles Vignoles.

In the seventeenth and eighteenth centuries, roads and other local projects were the concern of the grand juries. These bodies consisted of twenty-three members, including at least one from each barony, and met twice a year for a few days before the spring and autumn assizes. Individuals could make presentments for local projects and, if these were approved by the Grand Jury, carry them out either directly or by contracts. An affidavit was then presented to a subsequent meeting of the Grand Jury concerning the completion of the project and the costs involved. The latter were then levied by means of the county cess.

Following the establishment of the Post Office as a monopoly in 1784, there were several acts of parliament relating to roads, notably the Post Roads Act of 1792, the Public Roads Act of 1796, and the Mail Coach Roads Act of 1805. The Grand Jury system became increasingly inefficient in its functions, not least because of the lack of supervisory staff trained and experienced in road construction. An attempt was made in 1817 to improve the situation in this latter respect. The Grand Jury (Ireland) Act of 1817, which was strenuously resisted by the Irish MPs, provided for the appointment of county surveyors. A panel consisting of Thomas Telford (engineer to the Commission for Highland Roads and engineer to the Holyhead Road Commission), Alexander Taylor (author with his brother of the 1778 map of Irish Roads and planner and engineer for the Military Road in County Wicklow), and Francis Johnson (leading architect of public buildings), was appointed to examine and report on the large number of candidates for these positions. The panel concluded that none of the candidates had the required knowledge and experience of road-making and bridge-building that formed the greater part of the duties involved. As a consequence, the 1817 Act could not be implemented and, despite calls by a number of Select Parliamentary Committees, the situation was not rectified until 1833. Under the 1833 Act, the selection of county surveyors was assigned to the newly established Board of Public Works (Ireland).

The panel appointed consisted of Colonel John Fox Burgoyne (Chairman of the Commissioners), John Radcliff (Commissioner), and Jacob Owen (engineer and architect to the Board). They established a rigorous system of written examinations and interviews, which occupied nine hours per day for a full two weeks. They recommended a list of candidates they considered qualified, apparently in order of their suitability. It would appear that this was the first example of a written examination in connection with a public appointment in these islands.

The transition from surveying and canal engineering to road-making and railway construction in the second quarter of the nineteenth century may be illustrated by considering the career of William Dargan. Born in 1799 at Ardristan near Tullow in County Carlow, he went to school in Carlow town and then served a term of apprenticeship with a local surveyor. Sir Henry Parnell recommended him to Thomas Telford who employed him as an overseer on a section of the Holyhead Road. On his return to Ireland, Dargan began his career as an engineering contractor. One of his earliest contracts was for the construction of a road from Dublin to Howth, including a long sea wall at Sutton. His early contracts included work on the Ulster Canal and on the Kilbeggan branch of the Grand Canal.

His main contribution, however, was in relation to the rapidly expanding rail network in Ireland. The first of these lines for which Dargan contracted to build was that linking Dublin with the royal harbour at Kingstown (now Dún Laoghaire), opened in 1834. During the next 20 years, Dargan was responsible for building the main lines between Dublin and Cork, Dublin and Drogheda, Dublin and Wicklow and from Mullingar to Galway. He was responsible for promoting and largely financing the Exhibition of Irish Industry, held in Dublin in 1853, which reflected the changes in the Irish economy over the first half of the nineteenth century.

Developments in civil engineering and other branches of engineering during the second half of the nineteenth century and in the twentieth century may be traced in the published *Transactions of the Institution of Civil Engineers of Ireland* (commenced 1845) and later the *Engineers Journal*.

Mechanical and Mining Engineering

During the Middle Ages and the Renaissance, mechanical engineering was an integral part of general engineering, whether practised by military or civil engineers. The eighteenth century saw the emergence of the steam engine, which was to play such a large part in the Industrial Revolution. It is worth mentioning that the principal application of steam power in those early days was in mining engineering, which was an integral part of mechanical engineering. Throughout most of the seventeenth century, there was an interest in using steam to raise water. Robert Hooke (1635–1703) and Denis Papin (1647–1714) reported on their experiments to the Royal Society. In 1695, Thomas Savery (1650–1715), a military engineer and inventor, was granted a patent for 'a new invention for raising water … by the impellent force of fire'. He described his pump in a contribution to the Royal Society in 1699 and an improved version in a publication entitled *The Miner's Friend* in 1702. In the eighteenth century, the emergence of the steam engine led to a new era in mechanical engineering and in industry.

Early model of Trevithick steam locomotive.

The start of this transformation resulted from individual ironworkers with a background of craft training. Thomas Newcomen (1664–1729), the inventor of the stationary atmospheric steam engine, has been described as a practical tradesman and an ironworker. Around 1710, Newcomen experimented with a steam engine quite different from that of Savery and this appears to have been demonstrated in London around 1712. It is interesting to note that Newcomen's collaborators in the development and the early users of the engine were his nonconformist co-religionists. Thus the environment for the diffusion of his invention was markedly different from the environment of the Royal Society or the Smeatonian Dining Club.

By the early nineteenth century, engineers specialising in machines and the production of power had become more numerous and more influential. The monopoly of the Institution of Civil Engineers of London in regard to professional engineering in England was modified by the rise of the Institution of Mechanical Engineers and of the Institution of Electrical Engineers. The Institution of Mechanical Engineers was founded in Birmingham in 1847 and opened a headquarters in that city in 1851, by which time the membership had reached over 2,000. The idea is said to have arisen earlier that year when a number of engineers engaged on inspection of railway works had to take shelter from a severe rainstorm. In the discussion that followed, the question was raised that George Stephenson had been refused membership of the Civils unless he undertook to provide an essay as evidence of his engineering ability. There is no documentary evidence for this alleged slight to the most eminent of mechanical engineers of the day. However, over a century later, an Irish engineer who was a Fellow of the Institution of Civil Engineers of Ireland and a professor in an Irish University was required to write an essay before undergoing the professional interview for membership!

George Stephenson was the first President of the Institution of Mechanicals and was succeeded by his son, Robert, who was President from 1849 until 1853, and a few years later elected President of the Institution of Civil Engineers. The purpose of the Institution of Mechanical Engineers was described as follows: 'To enable mechanics and engineers in the different Manufactures, Railways and other Establishments in the Kingdom to meet and correspond, and by a mutual exchange of ideas respecting improvements in the various branches of Mechanical Science, to increase their knowledge and give an impulse to inventions likely to be useful to the world.'

In the same way as mechanical engineers felt that their professional needs and concerns were not catered for by the Institution of Civil Engineers, so too naval architects, mining engineers and marine engineers felt the need in the second half of the century to create their own professional bodies outside the structure of the Institution of Mechanical Engineers.

The naval architects were the first specialised group who found that their interests were not served by either the established Institution of Civil Engineers or the newly formed Institution of Mechanical Engineers. Their technology was rapidly changing because the traditional expertise of wooden vessels propelled by sail was being replaced by ironclads propelled by steam. In 1860, the Institution of Naval Architecture was formed 'to advance the science and the art of Naval Architecture'. This objective was stated more specifically in the Charter of 1910 as 'the improvement of ships and all that specially appertains to them, and the management of periodical meetings for the purpose of discussing practical and scientific subjects bearing upon the design and construction of ships and their means of propulsion and all that relates thereto'. An important feature of this institution was that, besides providing for the election of naval architects as members, it encouraged the recruitment of those skilled in the relevant crafts essential in shipbuilding.

Mining engineering has a long history — from 3000 BC in Egypt to the present day. During the Middle Ages the development of machines and the introduction of black powder into Europe were quickly availed of in mining operations. In the nineteenth century, mining operations were facilitated by the introduction of the steam drill, by Richard Trevithick, in 1813, followed by the piston drill in 1843, and by a new and improved pumping technology in Germany in 1853. Until 1887, mining engineers were catered for by the Institution of Mechanical Engineers and by a number of local institutes, but growing dissatisfaction with their position led to the founding of a separate Institution of Mining Engineers, in 1889. This caters for all engineers engaged in exploration, mineral separation, hydrometallurgy, electrical reduction, smelting and refining.

A separate Institution of Marine Engineers was founded in 1889 because it was felt that the interests of members were not catered for by either the Institution of Mechanical Engineers or the Institution of Naval Architects. It emphasised considerations beyond those of the traditional institutions when it stated in the invitation to the foundation meeting: 'It has been considered highly desirable to form an Institute and Club for Marine Engineers, having as its objects the promotion of those intellectual and social qualities which render life more honourable and pleasant by their possession'. The Institute catered for both sea-going and land-based marine engineers.

Nineteenth-Century Telegraph and Electrical Engineering

The emergence of electrical engineering as a separate discipline followed a somewhat different path from that of mechanical engineering. Mechanical engineering emerged largely as the result of a process based on experience, adaptation and invention. In the case of electrical engineering, the process was more akin to the modern sequence of scientific discovery, application to practical problems and innovation.

Though the control of electrical currents 'for the use and benefit of man' did not emerge until the nineteenth century, the natural phenomena of lightning and magnetism were obviously well known long before that time. Attempts to direct lightning by swords or by sharp ornaments on rooftops are recorded from classical times but systematic study dates only from Benjamin Franklin and others in the middle of the eighteenth century. Magnetism had been used for practical purposes long before this. The records of many classical civilisations record the use of a floating needle or of a lodestone for navigation on land or sea. The first application of magnetism to magic tricks, direction finding and games arose in China and later spread to the west. Columbus noted the variation in the deviation of the magnetic north from the geographic pole as he moved westward across the Atlantic at the end of the fifteenth century.

The birth of electrical engineering as a discipline is interesting not least because, like civil engineering, it involved development in the transition from the military use to more general use of various devices to transmit information rapidly from place to place. A pioneer in the classical method of semaphore signalling was Richard Lovell Edgeworth (1744–1817) who in 1767 proposed the use of the arms of windmills to convey the results of horse races from Newmarket to London, and resumed his experiments in 1794 to apply it for military purposes. The early history of the electric telegraph is a somewhat confused account of sporadic experiments. Francis Romalds (1788–1873) devised in 1816 an ingenious and robust system of electric telegraph but the Admiralty rejected his proposal. There were several subsequent developments culminating in the five-needle telegraph of Charles Wheatstone (1802–1875) and the polarised relay of Karl William Siemens (1823–1883), widely used by the postal authorities in Britain, as well as the earlier work in America of Samuel Morse and Alfred Vail.

Unlike civil and mechanical engineering, where the roots go back to the beginning of history, the evolution of electrical engineering dates back only to the first systematic experiments on magnetism by William Gilbert in the sixteenth century and Robert Boyle in the seventeenth century. Dunsheath (1962) in his *History of Electrical Engineering* includes an extensive chronological table covering the development of the understanding of electrical phenomena and their harnessing for useful purposes from AD 1269 to AD 1961. Every few years showed

Electricity generating station for Dublin's first trams.

a significant development in understanding or application. Highlights of nineteenth-century developments included the voltaic pile, announced by Volta (1745–1827) in 1800. In 1808, Humphrey Davy (1778–1829) demonstrated spectacular results on electro-chemical phenomena at a Royal Institution Lecture in London. In 1820, Ampere (1775–1836) communicated some important results on electrical phenomena to the French Academy of Science and, in 1831, Michael Faraday (1791–1867) discovered electro-magnetic induction. In 1842, Morse transmitted signals from one bank of a river to the other, whilst, in 1856, Lord Kelvin (1824–1907) developed the theory of the submarine cable. In 1875, electricity was first used to power furnaces. In 1881, the first hydroelectric power station was brought into operation at Niagara Falls on the US–Canadian border. In 1891, the National Physical Laboratory was established in Britain and, in 1897, Guglielmo Marconi (1874–1937) transmitted radio signals across the English Channel.

In London, in 1837, William Strogean, a cobbler interested in electrical experimentation, founded an Electrical Society, a move that was supported by Faraday amongst others. Unfortunately this venture was terminated in 1843, apparently because of the adoption of an over-ambitious programme which failed for lack of funds. It was not until 1871 that the forerunner of the present-day Institution of Electrical Engineers was established and electrical engineering came of age as a professional vocation. A group of eight engineers met in May 1871 and proposed a meeting with the following purpose: 'To consider the experiment of forming a Society of Telegraph Engineers, having for its object the general advancement of Electrical and Telegraph Science and more particularly for facilitating the exchange of information and ideas among its Members.'

This meeting was duly held and the society formed. Siemens, whose background was in the electrical industry, was its first president. The original requirement for membership was fixed as pupillage for five years in a responsible position, a reflection of the education and training of many engineers at the time. In 1889, the Institution of Telegraph Engineers became the Institution of Electrical Engineers and it received its Royal Charter in 1921.

In 1899, local sections of the IEE were established in Dublin, Glasgow, Newcastle-upon-Tyne and Cape Town. The Dublin Section was renamed as the Irish Centre in 1918 and as the Irish Branch in 1953. A Northern Ireland subcommittee was established in 1938 and became the Northern Ireland Centre in 1945.

The Institution of Radio and Electronic Engineers was founded in 1925 and received its Royal Charter in 1961. Its foundation and rapid growth had a military background because of the expansion of the use of radio in the First World War and of radar in the Second World War.

Further Differentiation

During the second half of the nineteenth century and the first half of the twentieth century, there was further specialisation in the engineering profession. This evolutionary process involved differences in engineering practices, evolving training and teaching systems, and in the separate development of the new engineering institutions. Whilst the first two processes were gradual, the third can be dated from the foundation of these separate institutions.

Between 1914 and 1979, the number of engineers represented by professional institutions had risen from 4,000 members of seventeen professional institutions to almost 400,000 members of a far wider variety of institutions. Members of the sixteen professional institutions had achieved Charter status. A search today on the Internet under the heading of 'engineering institutions' results in a list of 35 organisations recognised by the Engineering Council.

The variation in the membership of these various institutions over the past two centuries reflects the history of technology. Reference has already been made to the foundation of the institutions of Naval Architecture and of Mining Engineering. An example of a smaller institution is the Institution of Gas Engineers. In the first half of the nineteenth century, the number of public gas works in Britain grew to around 1,000. Later the use of gas spread from public lighting to domestic cooking and central heating. Shortly after the middle of the nineteenth century, moves towards forming a society for gas managers and engineers developed first in Scotland. In 1863, a group of gas engineers and gasworks managers met in Manchester and founded the British Association of Gas Managers, under the presidency of Thomas Hawksley, a well-known civil engineer. In 1888, the name was changed to The Gas Institute, but the desire for a strictly engineering body was reflected by the subsequent establishment of the Incorporated Institution of Gas Engineers, which received a Royal Charter in 1929.

A more specialised example of such integration was the unification in 1976 of the Institution of Heating and Ventilating Engineers (founded in 1897) and the Illuminating Engineering Society (founded in 1909), to form what is now known under its Royal Charter by the name of the Chartered Institution of Building Services Engineering (CIBSE).

Chemical engineering is founded on the changes in the nature and processing of raw materials in the eighteenth century, but did not evolve into a separate professional discipline until the beginning of the twentieth century. Up to the end of the seventeenth century, timber was the widely used material but at that time a combination of timber scarcity and increasing demand for raw materials led to technological innovations in iron working. Other developments in the eighteenth century were improvements in methods of evaporation in the salt industry and in the sugar industry, in distillation techniques, and in the development of unit operations in chemical industry. The transformation of the chemical industry from local small-scale enterprises to large-scale manufacture based on continuous processes in the nineteenth century led to the emergence of chemical engineering as a distinct discipline.

Chemical engineering is concerned with unit operations and covers a wide field, including oil engineering, materials, fertilisers and pharmaceuticals, as well as aspects of energy and environmental issues. The development of chemical engineering as a separate discipline occurred earlier in Germany and in the United States than in Britain. The American Institute of Chemical Engineering was founded in 1908, but the Institution of Chemical Engineers in the UK was not founded until the early 1920s.

In 1918, the Society of Chemical Industry in Britain established an engineering group, and the Institution of Chemical Engineers was founded in 1922. A Department of Applied Chemistry (later the Department of Chemical Engineering) was established at the Massachusetts Institute of Technology (MIT) in 1907. Postgraduate courses in chemical engineering were started in Britain in the 1920s. The first professorship in chemical engineering was established at Imperial College London in 1923 and an undergraduate course was established there in 1937.

The case of the professional organisation of agricultural engineering followed a path similar to that of chemical engineering. The American Society of Agricultural Engineers (ASAE) was founded in 1907. The chief mover behind the foundation was the 27-year-old J. Brownlee Davison who was Professor and Head of Agricultural Engineering at Iowa State College in Ames (Iowa). In Britain, the mechanisation of agriculture and the professionalisation of agricultural engineering developed more slowly. Although the Royal Agricultural Society of England was founded in 1838, almost 100 years elapsed before the foundation of the Institution of British Agricultural Engineers was founded in 1938. In 1924, Oxford University had established the Oxford Institute for Research in Agricultural Engineering but the National College for Agricultural Engineering (later Silsoe College) was established only in 1955.

In the first quarter of the twentieth century, efforts were made in the US. to offset the increasing differentiation in

at 41 Upper Sackville Street (as O'Connell Street in Dublin was then named). This change proved a strain on the resources of the organisation, partially due to the cost of furnishing the new premises, and maintenance charges out of all proportion to the size of the membership. Membership had been falling because of a change in government policy at the time and the lessening of the provision for public works, and consequently lack of work for engineers in Ireland.

Although many administrative and structural problems had arisen, the essential aims and objects of the founders were being fulfilled. Meetings were held frequently and papers presented and discussed. A good deal of time was devoted to the description of models and to the demonstration of engineering instruments, as the era of technical journals and commercial shows and exhibitions was in its infancy. Through the generosity of individual members, there was already a considerable accumulation of books and models for which rooms had to be provided and a curator appointed. Sadly, the models were later dispersed and only remnants of the library collection have survived to form an archive, now housed at 45 Merrion Square under an arrangement with the Irish Architectural Archive.

The Transactions (technical papers) of the ICEI were first published at the end of the session 1844–45 and have continued in an unbroken sequence up to the present day, apart from the period from 1972 to 1984 during which economic cutbacks resulted in the Transactions being archived but not published. Happily, that situation was rectified and the Transactions continue to provide a valuable record of engineering achievement in Ireland and elsewhere. They contain an impressive record of the contribution that engineers have made to the economy, to the welfare of the community, and to the country as a whole.

The perilous seven years with headquarters at Sackville Street were ended by a most magnanimous gesture by the Board of Trinity College Dublin who undertook, at the request of the Professor of Civil Engineering, Samuel Downing, to house and safeguard the collection of models and library items and to provide suitable rooms for council and general meetings, including fuel and light, free of charge and without limitation as to period.

Trinity College was to be used for the meetings of the ICEI for the next 30 years, whilst the Council considered ways of providing for an office and library in a business part of town. In due course, apartments were rented in the upper part of 136 St Stephen's Green West, which was accomplished by a combination of increasing members' subscriptions and a bequest of £1,200 (together with a collection of professional books), received under the will of a Past-President, Michael Bernard Mullins.

The Charter

The five years, from January 1874 to November 1879, when the Reading Room and Offices were located at St Stephen's Green, marked a most significant phase in the history of the ICEI, for it was during this period that it was granted a Royal Charter of Incorporation, thus giving it real status as a body entitled to represent and act for the engineering profession in Ireland.

The necessity of obtaining a Charter had been felt since the inception of the ICEI, and the granting of a Charter in 1877 marked a new phase in its growth. The then President, Robert Manning (1816–1897), the government drainage engineer whose research led him to derive the 'Manning Formula for Open Channel Flow', was named in the Charter together with others who 'have formed themselves into a Society for promoting the acquisition of that species of knowledge which appertains to the professions of Civil and Mechanical Engineers, and for the advancement of Engineering and Mechanical Science'. It will be observed that the original Charter stated that the objects were the advancement of Engineering Science as well as Mechanical Science, which latter was alone mentioned in the 1844 constitution, whilst the profession of Mechanical Engineer is mentioned for the first time. This may be accounted for by the fact that several prominent mechanical engineers were members of the Council at that time, but in any case it would seem as if it were intended that two distinct professions would be catered for by the one organisation. The retention of the word 'Civil' in the name appears to reflect the meaning of the word, which encompassed at that time mechanical sciences, rather than the exclusion of what is now a sister profession.

In his presidential address in that same year, Manning alluded to the role of the ICEI and the essentials of a profession when he said:

> Firstly it should be recognised and distinguished by the chief authority in the State: secondly, it should elect and if need be expel its own members; thirdly, it should have authority to make its own laws and have the power to enforce them; fourthly it should have a corporate existence, and lastly, it should have the power to determine who are qualified to practise, to grant diplomas to those who are and to forbid those who are not. All these belong to the profession of law and physic — all these we now possess, except the last. We have not sought it — we do not require it. If we possessed it, it would be nearly impossible to exercise it. Who shall define the boundaries of our profession, where the proper functions of the engineer begin or where they end? We have other and better uses for our Charter than to hinder anyone who chooses to apply his head or his hands for 'the use and convenience of man'.

The wisdom and foresight of those who sought and obtained the Charter ensured the independence of the profession and control by its own members, a matter that was also dear to the heart of Thomas Telford who said that, 'In foreign countries similar establishments are instituted by Government and their members and proceedings are under its control'.

The fundamental principles set out in the original Charter stood the test of time and continued to be valid and applicable under the Constitutions of 1922 and 1937 by virtue of the Adaptation of Charters Act 1926 that provided, *inter alia*, that any board or body governed by Charter shall be deemed a board or body constituted by statute.

By the mid-twentieth century, the profession of engineering had so advanced and the scope of engineering science had become so enlarged that the definition in the original Charter required extension. Furthermore, the management of the affairs of the ICEI demanded a larger and more representative Council. The Institution of Civil Engineers of Ireland (Charter Amendment) Act 1960 provided for a Council, exclusive of officers, of not fewer than 21 persons nor more than the number prescribed in the bylaws, in contrast to eight in the original Charter, together with all Past-Presidents. The number of these was reduced to not fewer than four to be appointed by the Council.

The purpose of the ICEI was redefined as for 'the promotion of that species of knowledge which appertains to the

Left: ICEI headquarters at 35 Dawson Street, Dublin; Above: ICEI Lecture Hall in Dawson Street, Dublin.

profession of Engineering and the special advancement of Engineering Science'. The word 'Civil' was to remain in the Institution's title for another decade, although its application extended far beyond the narrow confines of civil engineering.

Within two years of the granting of the Charter, the ICEI once again found itself in difficulties with accommodation. The lease of the house at St Stephen's Green had expired and the landlord's requirements for renewal were unacceptable. Ultimately, a short unexpired term of the interest of the lease of 35 Dawson Street was purchased. Some of the rooms were already let to tenants and there was a garden with stables at the rear that was eventually to become the site for a new Lecture Hall and Supper Room. The Office and Library were transferred to Dawson Street at the end of 1879, but the general meetings of the ICEI were still held in Trinity College.

The members felt that the progress of the ICEI was being retarded and its usefulness greatly lessened by the fact that the general meetings were not held in a hall connected with the headquarters of the organisation. Eventually, a hall was built in the rear garden of the Dawson Street premises and the first general meeting to be held there was on the evening of 16 December 1891, when the grateful thanks of the ICEI were again tendered to the Provost and Fellows of Trinity College for their hospitality in affording the organisation facilities for holding its meetings within the college for such a long period. The Supper Room was added in 1899. Meetings were held here in the Hall on the first Monday of the month from November to May when learned papers on a variety of engineering topics were delivered and discussed, that is, except for the presidential address, a custom first introduced in 1856, from which, according to precedent and practice, discussion is precluded.

The years at Dawson Street witnessed an almost continuous, if not steady, growth in membership and an upward trend in the standards demanded for membership. The extent to which the ICEI served its founders' main purpose of providing for personal interaction and mutual communication between the members may be judged by the contributions to be found in the Transactions. Many members contributed greatly to the progress of engineering science; others had an influence on the advancement of the prosperity and the economic development of this country. That the activities of the ICEI were not confined entirely to purely academic matters is evidenced by the publication, in 1928, of the *Scale of Fees and Conditions of Engagement*. This publication, and its subsequent revisions, proved of inestimable value to both consultants and clients in the years following, until its use was discontinued under the provisions of the competition legislation, in affecting the material welfare of members engaged in private practice. In addition, the *Conditions of Contract for Works of Civil Engineering Construction* was drafted and published at about the same time. It has since been updated and revised a number of times and continues to be used widely on Irish construction projects.

The years following the Second World War were years of very rapid changes in the world. The growth in technology was phenomenal, and the advances in scientific knowledge and its application were widening the sphere of engineering. Thus, when it was realised that the administrative structure imposed on the ICEI by its Charter was proving to be inhibiting and the limitations of the definitions of engineering were inadequate for modern times, steps were taken to have the Charter updated. This led to the passing, in 1960, of the Charter Amendment Act. An enlarged Council with the involvement of many more members in the government of the ICEI had an immediate effect. The setting up of committees was now greatly facilitated with the increase of personnel and the presence of a young and vigorous membership.

Reorganisation

However, the most significant development, and the most dramatic in its consequences, was the setting up of a Policy Committee to consider the ways and means whereby the ICEI might serve the interests of members of all branches of engineering in Ireland. The committee investigated the benefits that engineers derived from the wide range of societies to which they contributed. Representatives of other engineering societies were consulted about the possibility of creating more dynamic engineering opinion and development in the country. Various study groups were set up to examine the best means of achieving unified representation for the engineering profession in Ireland on matters concerning professional standards and international mutual recognition under the Treaty of Rome and the EEC (now the EU) The effect of the newly created Council of Engineering Institutions (CEI) in the United Kingdom had also to be taken into account.

A special General Meeting of the Institution was held on 20 April 1964 at which a report was presented entitled 'Institution: A Unified Society Plan for Development 1964'. The report was adopted in principle and the Council was authorised to purchase a site for the construction of an Engineering Centre and the disposal of the premises at 35 Dawson Street.

The policy for developmental expansion was presented to a wider audience at a Conversazione held on 3 December 1964 in Dawson Street in the presence of An Taoiseach, Sean Lemass, and a number of distinguished guests from the Department of State, educational bodies, industry leaders and kindred professional bodies.

In order to cater for the needs of all engineering disciplines in the country, it was stated that the intention of the Institution was to seek an Act to change its name to 'The Institution of Engineers of Ireland', and it was explained that, whilst up to that time, it had been open to all branches of the profession, it had catered mainly for the requirements of the civil engineering branch. So, it was felt necessary to seek the change of name in order to draw in a more widely based membership. The organisation was to become more deeply involved in assisting, through the development of technology, in the nation's economic and industrial growth by reorganising the structure of the engineering profession so as to embrace all its branches.

The disposal of the premises in Dawson Street was to lead to the building of or the acquisition of new modern premises and the setting up of an adequate Engineering Centre which, it was hoped, would be shared with Cumann na nInnealtóirí (CnaI), referred to hereafter as the Cumann. The Royal Institute of the Architects of Ireland had also expressed an interest in such a project. The centre was to provide a well-equipped modern lecture theatre as well as offices. The search for a building or a site proved to be a very long and fruitless task. The government vetoed what was considered to be an ideal site, whilst other sites failed to be granted planning permission on appeal.

When, at this Conversazione, the two distinct functions of the ICEI as a 'learned society', and the Cumann catering for the good of engineers collectively and individually, were clearly enunciated, the hope was expressed that one day the two bodies might draw closer together. By 1963, a joint committee of the two bodies had reported.

Cumann na nInnealtóirí (The Cumann)

We should now retrace our steps to examine the foundations of the Cumann.

The decade of the 1920s was a difficult time in Ireland as the country recovered from Civil War and the divisions, political and social, occasioned by that conflict cast their shadow over economic and social life. The decade was, however, brightened considerably by the commencement of the Shannon Scheme which was a major and courageous undertaking for such a young state and which was internationally recognised as a major engineering achievement.

At that time also, many young engineers who were concerned at the inadequate salaries and conditions of employment of many members of their profession decided to form an organisation for professional engineers dedicated to the improvement of the standing, status and remuneration of the profession in Ireland. The reason for an organisation separate from the Institution of Civil Engineers of Ireland (ICEI) was that the Council of the ICEI considered that its Charter precluded it from negotiating on conditions of employment. Nevertheless, the ICEI's premises were made available for a meeting on the 27 February 1928, at which it was decided to establish a new organisation with the simple overall objective 'to improve and advance the status and remuneration of qualified members of the Engineering Profession in Ireland'.

At this meeting, two people from outside the engineering profession were present as advisers. They were Dr Hennessy of The Irish Medical Association, and solicitor Sean Ó hUadhaigh, who acted as Honorary Secretary and who offered the use of his office for future meetings. He subsequently gave sterling service to the Cumann throughout its formative years. Thus, Cumann na nInnealtóirí came into being.

The early years were difficult. Membership was relatively small and funds were never adequate. The Council of the Cumann consisted of young engineers — there was no office, no secretarial staff and no journal. Communication was by personal letter, followed subsequently by circulars produced on a duplicator. That the Cumann survived at all was a miracle and a tribute to the courage, energy and initiative of the founders and also to their wisdom in setting a course and pursuing objectives that inspired their successors during the subsequent decades. Their work was crowned in the unification of the Irish engineering profession in 1969, when the administration and structure of the Cumann, which had developed so well in the previous decades, provided much of the bedrock administration and structure of the unified Institution of Engineers of Ireland (IEI).

By 1930, the Cumann, advised by Ó hUadhaigh, had prepared a draft Registration Bill for the engineering profession and presented it to government. Independently, the ICEI prepared a similar draft bill. The then Minister for Industry and Commerce rejected both drafts and suggested that both organisations agree a draft bill on which progress might eventually be made. This proved to be an unrequited hope during the subsequent decades.

In the early years of its existence, the Cumann made an arrangement with the Electric Power Engineers Association who agreed that, for a share of the subscription, they would handle all negotiations for salaries and conditions of employment. This arrangement was terminated in 1936, which was a sign of the growing maturity and confidence of the Cumann. Although there were no spectacular achievements in the negotiation field, much work was done quietly by regular communication with employers and government departments. The tactic was developed of following up an advertisement that offered an inadequate salary with another which asked intending applicants to seek the advice of the Cumann before applying. This proved very effective. At the same time, recommended salaries for various degrees of experience were developed and brought to the notice of employers.

In 1937, a register of engineers in Ireland was compiled which included 1,392 names. The membership of the Cumann was 90 in 1936, 192 in 1937, 254 in 1938, and had risen to 363 by 1939.

Until 1938, the Cumann had no fixed abode and in that year an office was rented at 1–3 Westmoreland Street in Dublin from Kevan & Sons, Chartered Accountants, and this was to be the Cumann's address until 1950.

The Secretary of the Cumann, J.G. Charlton, resigned in 1940 and Kevan & Sons were appointed Secretaries to the Cumann, which task was assigned to Eileen Walshe, who maintained a valuable association with the Cumann until shortly before her death in 1967.

The lack of a suitable organ of communication had been a long-felt disadvantage and, in December 1940, the first issue of the *Engineers Journal* appeared — it was published initially as an annual, later as a quarterly, and subsequently in 1949 as a monthly publication. 'The Journal' as it is affectionately known, has, since then, provided innumerable articles on a comprehensive range of subjects pertaining to engineering history, education, practice and management, as well as a very wide range of engineering news, views, comment and special features Among the many authors who regularly contributed a variety of articles to the *Journal* were John Manning, Jock Harbison, Amhalaidh Ó hAonghusa, Ron Cox, Redmond Holloway, Finbar Callanan and Alf Kelly. However, the main strength of the *Journal* was that it provided the engineering profession with a popular and effective method of communication.

In 1939, a Memorandum, Articles of Association and By-laws were drafted under the guidance of Ó hUadhaigh. The aims of the Cumann were redefined and expanded. This new Constitution became effective in May 1941 and it governed the Cumann to the end of its existence.

In 1941, a Trade Union Bill was passed by Dáil Éireann making it illegal for any body, not being an exempted body, to carry out negotiations for the fixing of wages or conditions of employment unless such body was the holder of a negotiating licence. The Cumann became an exempted body by ministerial order and thus became empowered to negotiate on behalf of its members.

During the Second World War, the Cumann organised studies and talks and published pamphlets, particularly on the production and use of indigenous fuels, for which many of the members had responsibility in the Turf Development Board, local authorities and elsewhere.

An important initiative was undertaken in 1941 with the establishment of the Cork Region of the Cumann, and within a few years several other Regions had been established throughout the country. In 1946, the Regions were empowered to nominate representatives to the Central Council and the development of activities within the Regions, both technical and social, was a very important influence on the subsequent growth of the organisation, as well as in unifying the variety of disciplines of the profession for which the Cumann catered.

Registration continued to be a live issue in the 1940s. A joint committee of the Cumann and the ICEI on behalf of engineers and the Royal Institute of the Architects of Ireland prepared reciprocal Draft Registration Bills. However, once again it proved a fruitless exercise.

By 1949, the Cumann was a sound and thriving organisation and was proving very successful in advancing the interests of the profession in all its vocations and disciplines. In contrast to the early years, it had garnered the support of many senior engineers who gave unstinting service as Council members, as officers and as active members of the vari-

Headquarters of the Irish Engineering Profession at 22 Clyde Road, Dublin.

ous vocational groups and committees. The willingness of eminent members of the profession, such as Professor Felix Hackett, Nicholas O'Dwyer, Dr Thomas McLaughlin and Professor Harry Walsh to be presidents of the Cumann in its early years was a very significant influence in establishing the credibility of the organisation, not only within the profession, but also with those with whom the Cumann was negotiating or communicating.

In 1950, the Cumann moved to rented office accommodation at 59 Merrion Square, which was the nearest it had come to having a headquarters. However, it was considered that a proper headquarters should be acquired that would provide adequate office accommodation, meeting rooms, room for development, and a club for members. Accordingly, in 1955, the very fine premises at 22 Clyde Road, in Dublin 4, was purchased. It was renovated and fitted out through the enthusiastic voluntary efforts of many members of the profession, led by the Chairman of the Central Council, A.F. McGeorge. In light of the subsequent unification of the profession, it is of interest to note some lines of verse composed by the ESB engineer and *Engineers Journal* correspondent John Manning, who, in reference to the new headquarters, wrote

> Well I declare
> The Engineers are going to migrate from Merrion Square...
>
> Well I guess, the crowd up in Dawson Street
> Will envy us our new dwelling
> They may even want to join with us someday
> There's no telling....

At that stage of the growth and development of the Cumann, considerable progress had been made in fulfilling its objective of advancing the standing, status and remuneration of members of the profession. This work was pursued actively by the system of vocational groups, which represented the various areas of employment, and which had developed over the years. Notable amongst the groups in question were those representing engineering personnel in the ESB, the local authorities, the Defence Forces (engineer officers only), Bord na Móna, Posts and Telegraphs, Aer Lingus and CIE.

In addition, the Cumann played a very positive role in furthering the interests of smaller groups and individuals for whom negotiating services were supplied. Remuneration was consistently improved and, without question, the efforts of the Cumann in its formative years, and subsequently, played a very significant part in advancing the cause of engineering in Ireland and in projecting the profession as a rewarding career to be sought and followed.

The Regions were particularly valuable sounding boards for the members throughout the country, where ideas were generated, proposals were made, and grievances and queries aired. It was a significant strength of the Cumann that it was in constant communication with its members, and its ability to deal with bread-and-butter issues, as well as furthering a wide range of policy issues and educational and social events, was a unifying influence which added greatly to its growth throughout the 1950s and 1960s in particular.

It was the tradition of the Cumann, in its negotiations in relation to salaries and conditions of employment, to eschew industrial action, not only because it was not a trade union, but also because many members considered quite seriously that industrial action could be unethical as far as the practice of their profession was concerned. Up to a point, employers respected this attitude. However, as time moved on in the late 1950s and particularly during the 1960s, it became apparent to many in some employments that in the more difficult era of industrial relations that was developing in Ireland and elsewhere at that time, there was a grave danger of being left behind in terms of salary progression unless negotiations could be backed up by the threat of or by the actuality of effective industrial action.

The first approach by the Cumann to industrial action was in 1953 when the post of County Engineer of Dublin was advertised at a downgraded salary. The Cumann succeeded in getting all applicants to agree to withdraw their applications, and thus began what became known as 'the ban' ('boycott' would probably have been a better word). By 1956, posts of County and City Engineer and some Chief Assistant posts had been affected by the ban in seven local authorities. There were mixed feelings about this action and it was a contentious issue. Eventually a referendum of local authority engineers in 1958 recommended the lifting of the ban. This was not done before an Extraordinary General Meeting (the first in Cumann history) had been called on a motion to disregard the referendum and hold a new one involving all Cumann members. The motion was lost.

The negotiation services of the Cumann were availed of largely by engineers in the public sector and, in that regard, the ESB and the local authorities were the leaders. In effect, the scales negotiated for those two vocations generally set the standard for the remuneration of engineers throughout the public sector and, in very many cases, in the private sector also.

As it grew in numbers and influence, the Cumann also strengthened its links with the Institution of Civil Engineers of Ireland, The Engineers Guild (the UK counterpart of the Cumann), the Irish branches of the British Engineering Institutions (particularly the IEE and the IMech E) and especially with the Irish Medical Association, whose aims and objectives on behalf of its members mirrored those of the Cumann. These contacts were very valuable, not only in broadening the Cumann's influence within its own professional group of members, but also in learning from others, such as the medical profession, who had been involved with the Cumann since its foundation.

In that regard, in 1961, an Industry Committee was set up by the Cumann to cater specifically to the need of engineers in industry, and subsequently an Engineering Development Council was established between the Cumann, the Federation of Irish Industry, and the trade unions, with the objective of furthering dialogue with regard to engineering development in Ireland.

An engineering voice and influence in government, and in politics generally, was considered of great importance to the profession and the Cumann as a nominating body for elections to the Seanad actively supported the candidacy

the foundation meeting in the same location as 150 years previously. It was a year of constant activity, under the presidency of Robert Hayes, with over 30 individual events in Dublin alone, including a memorable McLaughlin Lecture given by Professor Sean de Courcy, entitled 'A History of Irish Engineering' and which forms the basis of the introduction to this book. The Women in Engineering Year was launched in the following February. This was a very successful venture with a number of activities designed to advance engineering as a very appropriate career choice for women, including seminars and talks by prominent women engineers, media presentations, and the issue of a special postage stamp by An Post. In 1986, just four per cent of the IEI membership was women, although the numbers studying engineering were approaching 15 per cent of the engineering student population.

As the 1990s approached, a major problem facing the IEI was the pressure on space in Clyde Road caused by the greatly increased activities and numbers of meetings, and also the increase in staff numbers occasioned by the expansion in membership. Accordingly, plans were made to build an Education Centre to the rear of the premises, incorporating a lecture theatre, a conference room and an extension to the Engineers Club restaurant. An economic recession meant that it was a difficult time to consider building, but the growth of the membership and the substantial support of fundraising activities by the Regions, the members, and a variety of firms, coupled with the close involvement of President, Sean Wallace, and President-Elect, Michael Higgins, encouraged the IEI to proceed with its plans, and the new complex with a 150-seat lecture theatre was opened in 1991 by the then Minister for the Environment, Pádraig Flynn. In the same year, the IEI was honoured by Mary Robinson, the newly elected President of Ireland, who agreed to accept Honorary Fellowship of the IEI.

In 1994, it was decided to avail of the opportunity to take a tenancy of the adjacent premises, number 23 Clyde Road, to provide additional office space for staff and to free up space in number 22 for meetings and courses.

Since unification, the IEI had sought to contribute as much as possible to the many areas of national concern where engineering was seen to have a significant role. Apart from its reports and representations to government with regard to matters of national policy where engineering was involved, the IEI also had a serious concern with manpower planning and the need to keep increasing the supply of engineering graduates at degree, diploma and certificate level. In that regard, it participated fully with the Royal Irish Academy (RIA), the NBST, and the Department of Labour in the manpower conferences of the early 1980s that proved so important in pointing the way to future developments.

At that time also, a very positive effort was made by the IEI, through its Young Engineers Section (founded in 1980), to project engineering to school-leavers through a series of well-attended lecture and demonstration events in TCD. These were a forerunner of a variety of events organised by the IEI in subsequent years in Dublin and in the Regions to further engineering as a career. Amongst school-leavers there was a greatly increased interest in engineering as a career and, even during the worst of the economic depression of the 1980s, there continued to be a great demand for places on engineering courses, which of course bore fruit in the eventual economic expansion of the 1990s.

Library and Archive

The Library and Archive at Clyde Road has over the years provided a service for members and researchers. Matthew (Matt) O'Donovan, in addition to his duties as Secretary, particularly on the learned body side of the Institution, had an abiding interest in its preservation and expansion. The one-time Honorary Librarian, Noel Hughes, devoted considerable time and effort over many years to the good order and cataloguing of the Library and his book, *Irish*

Engineering 1760–1960, drew considerably on the historic volumes and records of the library. Amongst those who made significant contributions to the work of the Library and Archive, were Past-President Peter O'Keeffe, Professor Sean de Courcy, Jock McEvoy, Ron Cox, Eoin Ó Cionna and the Librarian, John Callanan. Much of the archival material has now been transferred to the care of the staff of the Irish Architectural Archive in Dublin, where the material remains available to members.

The practice of the IEI Regions hosting the Annual Conference in turn, which commenced in Limerick in 1979 during the presidency of Morgan Sheehy, and continued in Kilkenny in 1980 under president Liam O'Brien, was a resounding success and both strongly furthered the concept. The practice did much to strengthen the Regions themselves and the contribution of the members to the organisation of IEI throughout the country. Major annual conferences have been held every year since then and have addressed a range of national issues.

The IEI continued to foster close relations with other professional bodies and trade associations in matters of common purpose, particularly in the construction industry. This has been particularly so in the case of the Association of Consulting Engineers in Ireland (ACEI), which body has at all times been fully supportive of the IEI and whose members have contributed significantly in time and involvement to its activities.

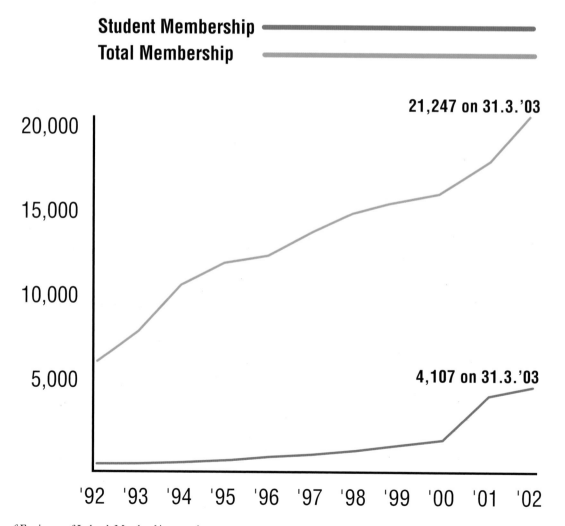

Institution of Engineers of Ireland: Membership growth 1992–2002.

Through the 1990s, the IEI expanded considerably as recruitment and new activities and services, coupled with an improving economy, saw membership increase to a total of 13,000 by 1996. Staff reorganisation resulted in the Director becoming Director-General, supported by four Directors appointed to be responsible for Education, Development, Finance, and Membership Qualifications, representing the prime administrative functions. The fundraising efforts of the previous years meant that the outstanding debt on the Education Centre had been paid off by 1997. At the end of March 1996, Finbar Callanan retired from the position of Director-General and was succeeded by Frank Burke.

The Academy of Engineering

Prior to his retirement, Callanan had made a proposal to the Council of the IEI that an all-Ireland Academy of Engineering be set up, its membership to be made up of the most senior and eminent engineers on the island of Ireland. The idea was that such an academy would harness the experience and wisdom of such members, many of them retired, and would provide a most useful and influential think-tank concerning matters in which engineering plays an important role. Elsewhere, such an academy had been formed in Britain in the early 1980s (The Royal Academy of Engineering). It had been most effective in its operations and had earned an enviable reputation for the work it produced. Similar academies had also been set up throughout Europe and further afield, all with the same concept of availing of the contributions of the most eminent and experienced engineers and applied scientists in the service of their respective countries. The proposal to set up the Irish Academy of Engineering (IAE) received enthusiastic support from former IEI Presidents, Liam Fitzgerald and John Killeen, as well as from IEI Honorary Members, Sir Bernard Crossland and Sir Philip Foreman, and from Gordon Millington, OBE, from Northern Ireland.

Killeen, who had worked very diligently to get the Academy up and running, was appointed its first President with Finbar Callanan being appointed Secretary. The IAE was formally launched on 26 May 1997 by Phillip Callery, the then President of the IEI. The Inaugural Address was given by Dr Tony Barry, Chairman of CRH plc, who spoke of the importance of the Academy in a developing technological economy and the contribution which it could make to engineering thinking and policy making in the Ireland of the future.

The IAE is a learned society of the engineering profession, the objective of which is 'to advance the science and practice of engineering in Ireland as an essential element in national development and the enhancement of living standards'. As an all-Ireland body, the Academy performs a most important role in linking the engineering profession in both jurisdictions on the island in matters of common interest affecting the island. It is a completely independent body with its own governing council and was established by the IEI to be so. The Academy continues to receive financial support from the IEI (now Engineers Ireland) to assist it in pursuing its objectives, and its administration is managed by the Association of Consulting Engineers of Ireland (ACEI), which provides secretarial and accountancy services and accommodation for meetings of the Academy.

Membership of the Academy is currently limited to 125. Nominees for membership must be shown to possess demonstrable achievement and eminence in their careers, and election to the Academy is recognised as a significant acknowledgement of such achievement and eminence.

In pursuit of its objectives, the Academy produces reports and commentaries on what it recognises as important and relevant topics on which it wishes to comment. These reports may be prepared either by the Academy acting on its own, or in conjunction with Engineers Ireland or other parties. Such reports have featured investment in education, spatial strategy, energy, transport, mathematics and management in engineering education, environment, and future industrial and economic development, among others. Such reports are widely circulated to government-elected representatives, and other organisations and individuals to whom such reports are deemed to be relevant.

The Academy is very active in the European Council of Applied Sciences and Engineering (Euro-Case) and maintains a close relationship with the Royal Academy of Engineering, with which it has exchanged study visits. It also maintains contact with the Swedish Academy whose structure may be a potential model for Ireland in the future.

The Academy seeks to maintain a close relationship with the two administrations on the island of Ireland and to be recognised as a valuable source of independent comment on matters of overall policy in Northern Ireland and in the Republic, in particular where engineering has an important role.

A Celebration of Irish Engineering

In 1996, the IEI organised a very successful series of events under the title of 'A Celebration of Irish Engineering'. The idea behind this celebration was to bring home to all sections of Irish society the past and present contributions of engineering to Irish life and national development. The 'Celebration' received encouraging support from academia and employers and was a significant boost to the IEI and to Irish engineering in general, as it tracked a course from a largely agricultural society to a new era when engineering could be seen as one of the main engines of change.

A feature of that time and succeeding years was the return to Ireland of many of the graduates who had emigrated in the 1970s and 1980s and who returned to Ireland enriched by the valuable international experience that they had garnered in the meantime and which contributed so much to the phenomenon of the 'Celtic Tiger'.

The launch of the Irish Academy of Engineering (IAE) in May 1997 by IEI President Philip Callery was a most significant event. It was a courageous and a very forward-looking initiative of the IEI to set up an independent sister organization, the purpose of which was to tap into the wisdom and experience of those engineers who in their careers had achieved well-recognized prominence in their chosen profession. There has since been very valuable interaction between both bodies in matters of common purpose.

Prior to his presidency, Callery devoted considerable time to the position of Chairman of the IEI Road Transportation Committee out of which a comprehensive series of submissions on road accidents were presented to government that presaged many of the actions taken by government in succeeding years to limit death on the roads. Others who gave very valuable service in this and other areas of transport policy were Past-Presidents Patrick Jennings and Richard Grainger, the Chief Civil Engineer and Chief Mechanical Engineer respectively of Irish Rail.

In 1997, Gordon Millington was elected President. He was the first member from Northern Ireland to occupy the position and his election was an appreciation of his work for the IEI throughout his career, not least in his efforts in furthering north-south relations and his major role with others in setting up the very successful Northern Ireland Region of the IEI, of which he was first Chairman. The Millington Report on Accreditation, which was revised under his chairmanship, was a very valuable exercise in updating the former procedures in the light of experience gained since the early 1980s.

New Corporate Plan

The growth of the economy was reflected in the continuing expansion of the IEI membership and its influence. In 1997, a steering group was established to oversee the workings of the IEI under the title of 'New Directions'. The impetus of the review was threefold. Firstly, it was felt that a root and branch review would be fruitful; secondly, in the light of a doubling of membership in the previous five years, to consider if it were possible to obtain a further doubling in the next five year period; and finally, it was felt that there was a need to review the purpose, governance and structure of the IEI to ensure its continuing relevance and success well into the next century. This strategic review and corporate plan was unveiled in May 1998 and subsequent years saw the vigorous implementation of the strategies that had been proposed.

Under the guidance of IEI President Jack Kavanagh, special emphasis was given to the promotion of the Chartered Engineer concept. Revised procedures for assessment for chartered status had been drawn up in the previous years and the value of the designation in enhancing the profession by the recognition of academic qualification, followed by well-attested experience and responsibility, was continually emphasized, not only to the proposed applicants, but also to all who had a concern for the education and post-graduate training of engineers.

Following the unification of the profession, the role of technician engineers and technicians within the IEI had received considerable attention. There was always a very strong realization that the availability of such graduates from the Colleges of Technology and the Regional Technical Colleges had been a significant plus in the development of modern Irish industry, and it had been the constant objective to enhance the appreciation of their skills, qualifications and status within the IEI and with industry and the public.

Associate Engineers

In that regard, Michael O'Donnell, Director of the College of Technology, Bolton St and a Past-President of the IEI had been a strong advocate of the need to accommodate technician engineers and technicians within the IEI's structure, and to recognize their qualifications and contribution within the family of engineering. His contribution was very great, as was his knowledge and advice as Chairman for many years of the Membership & Qualifications Board in assessing the great variety of qualifications of all candidates applying to the IEI for any of the grades of membership. He had strongly supported the AEng review committee, which had met under the chairmanship of Tim Corcoran, and which had produced a report on the procedures to be adopted for the award of the designatory title AEng (Associate Engineer) to those who had qualified with a three-year diploma in engineering, and who had appropriate and responsible engineering experience following graduation. Additionally, procedures for providing ladders of advancement from diploma to degree level for graduates, and who wished to avail of such opportunities, were reviewed and revised.

Continuing Professional Development

The implementation of the corporate plan set the scene for much of the IEI's activity as it moved into the next century. The programme of Continuing Professional Development (CPD) was instituted in 2000 and continued to expand. The IEI established strong links with industry and other organisations employing engineers and engineering technicians, with the objective of encouraging the development of vigorous and well-defined training programmes for their engineering personnel. These programmes would be accredited by the IEI, for their value in furthering the formation and contribution of engineers in the pursuit of their employment, and in their approach to chartered status. This was a most successful venture and the take-up by employers was most encouraging. In 2001, during the presidency of Liam Connellan, the Department of Trade and Employment agreed to provide matching funding for a three-year programme to accelerate the implementation of this CPD programme in the light of its national significance. Additionally in 2002, in pursuance of the Corporate Development Plan, the number of IEI Divisions was increased from 10 to 12 with the addition of an Information Division (ICT) and a new Local Government Division. These changes reflected the expansion in the nature, disciplines, requirements and volume of the membership.

Software Engineering

A historic step was taken in 2001 with the accreditation of the first four software engineering degree courses offered in Irish colleges. This was significant in that it marked the formal introduction of a new discipline to the IEI that allowed such graduates to apply for chartered membership. Much of the credit for these important developments must go to Professor Jane Grimson, the first lady president of the IEI, who worked diligently to forge a valuable Memorandum of Understanding between the IEI and the Irish Computer Society, thus ensuring that this new and important engineering discipline was appropriately recognized by the IEI.

Director-General Frank Burke had resigned from the IEI in 1999 to set up a private consultancy and, on his retirement was replaced temporarily by Past-President Pierce Pigott pending the appointment of a successor. During his tenure of office, Burke had done invaluable work, particularly in strengthening and expanding the international links of the IEI with FEANI and with the Washington Accord. He was also a founder member of the IAE.

In September 1999, Paddy Purcell was appointed Director-General and, until his retirement in 2004, served with

Paddy Purcell, Director-General, 1999–2004.

considerable dynamism and enterprise in implementing the corporate plan, which had proved of such benefit to the activities and governance of the IEI as it faced ever-changing challenges. A revised and comprehensive Code of Ethics was drawn up that received widespread favourable comment, and which set the ethical standards for the membership of the engineering institution to follow for many years ahead. Additionally, the corporate governance of the organisation continued to be strengthened and the public relations, particularly communication with the media, government, and the public were enhanced considerably.

5

ROADS

Peter O'Keeffe, Declan McIlraith & Billy McCoubrey

THE EARLIEST MENTION OF A SYSTEM of principal roads in Ireland is recorded as AD 123 in the *Annals of the Four Masters*, the entry indicating that the five principal roads to Tara of the Kings were classified and named Slighe Asail, Slighe Midhluachra, Slighe Cualann, Slighe Mór and Slighe Dála. An addendum suggests that the Slighe Mór coincided with a line called Escir Riada, which was identified as the boundary between the territory held by Conn, King of the northern Irish, called Leth Cuinn, and that held by Moga Nuadth, King of the southern Irish, called Leth Moga, after the battle of Moylena. The *Annals of Tighernach* record that this encounter took place AD 166. So began the history of Irish roads.

The ability of the Celts and earlier inhabitants to carry out large-scale construction works is evidenced by the dated prehistoric earthworks at Rathcroghan, Aileach, Emain Macha and many other sites. The recent finds of the plank road sections at Corlea and Derryaghan bogs in County Longford, dated to 148 and 156 BC, probably indicate an early attempt to build a road linking Rathcroghan and Uisneach via the Shannon ford 'Athleague' near the present village of Lanesborough. The work displayed an exceptional level of woodworking skill, but the useful life was short as the heavy oak planks sank into the deep bog when saturated and the ultimate answer was drainage and lightweight fill. As practically all journeys begin and end at habitations, the density and distributions of man-made features, such as ecclesiastical sites, castles and ring forts, suggest road corridors.

The end of the first millennium AD is an appropriate point at which to review the development of travel, transport, and the extension of the principal roads. The common Irish word for a road was 'Bóthar', the width of which was to be sufficient to enable two cows to fit upon it, one lengthwise, one athwart. It was so designated to protect a cow with its calf from being gored by a passing bull. The word 'Bealach' was used to describe a pass through a wood and wide enough for a packhorse. 'Slighe' seems to have been reserved for the network of routes described previously and the principal work in constructing them was cutting passes through the many woods and forests. Irish archaeological evidence for early wheeled vehicles is surprisingly rare, packhorses and bullocks being the usual carriers for travelling any distance.

The importance of river crossings was evidenced by special names: Áth Mor, Áth Trasna and so on. Six distinctive names were used for bridges: *cesaig droichet* for a wicker bridge, *cliath droichet* for a hurdle bridge, *clar droichet* for a timber bridge, *cloch droichet* for a stone bridge, *droichet clochaeltra* for a bridge of stone and mortar, and *droichet long* for a bridge of boats. Early mentions and descriptions of these are given in O'Keeffe and Simington (1991). For example, the face of Mabes Bridge in County Meath illustrates how the corbelled span as used in buildings may have evolved around the eleventh century into the radial arch.

There is a surprising lack of descriptions of the procedures, tools, materials and methods used in road construction in both Irish and English writings up the end of the fifteenth century. One notable exception is Cogitosus's seventh-century account of the life of St Brigid, translated by Canon O'Hanlon (1877). It describes how the local king commanded all the inhabitants of his territory (in Kildare) to assemble and take part in the construction of a new road. The same procedure was applied by the King of Munster to build bridges at Áth Caille and Killaloe in 1071.

The main obstacle to tracing the development of Ireland's road network has been the absence of early maps showing the roads before the seventeenth century. O'Keeffe (2001) compiled a composite map showing the principal natural physical features that affected roads, namely mountains above the 600 foot contours, the larger rivers, lakes and estuaries, and raised bogs. On this map, O'Keeffe superimposed the roads shown on other early maps and estimated that the principal road network AD 1169 would have been about 3,600 miles, although there were naturally many additional local, as distinct from principal, roads.

The Norman Invasion

The Anglo-Normans, on the invitation of Dermot McMurrough, King of Leinster, whose caput was in Ferns in County Wexford, landed at Bannow Bay in south Wexford in May 1169. They were closely followed in 1170 by Strongbow with an army of 200 knights and 1,000 infantry. Strongbow captured Waterford and then marched on Dublin. The English Henry I followed with another large army later in the same year. These invaders brought with them a new concept in relation to public roads, namely a law defining the King's highway or *via regia* as 'one which is always open and which no man may shut by any threats, as leading to a city, port or town'. The King's highway was also interpreted as a right of passage, as distinct from a specific way, such that, when the road became impassable because of flooding, rotting or other natural obstruction, the traveller could deviate on to another line, even if this meant crossing through tillage land.

Prince (later King) John spent part of 1185 in Ireland and returned in 1210. He was dubbed the 'Bridge Monarch' because of his initiative in ordering the erection of stone bridges over the larger rivers. For example, he ordered the building of Old Thomond Bridge over the Shannon at Limerick. This had fifteen pointed segmental arches and survived, albeit with many alterations at each end, until it was demolished and replaced in 1840.

By AD 1250, the Anglo-Normans held all the Norse ports, most of Leinster, Munster, Counties Antrim and Down, and a belt of land across the Midlands. The conclusion by many historians that this advance 'went too far too fast' is convincing evidence of the existence in 1169 and utility of the extensive principal road network then in existence. Apart from bridges and the cutting of passes through the woods, little written evidence of Anglo-Norman road building has been found. It seems that the barons were too preoccupied in developing the manors, which involved mainly local road construction.

Affairs in the Republic of Ireland. The Headquarters for Waterways Ireland is in Enniskillen, County Fermanagh, with regional offices located in Scarriff, County Clare, Carrick on Shannon, County Leitrim, and in Ashtown, County Dublin.

Early Navigations in Ireland

Ireland is well endowed with lakes, rivers and watercourses of all types, reflecting a relatively damp climate and low-lying nature of much of the terrain. It is customarily likened to a saucer with a rim of mountains (chipped where rivers escape to the sea) surrounding the central limestone plain. Heavy rainfall and poor drainage have turned much of the central plain into peat bog, formed by growth and decay of sphagnum moss and other plants. However, most Irish rivers were not easily navigable in their natural state, and various engineering solutions were advocated over the centuries to improve navigation.

In 1178, a very early piece of canal engineering took place when the friars of Claregalway Abbey became tired of the long detour they had to make and applied for permission to construct an artificial cut through an island to shorten their journey. In time, the Friar's Cut, became the main navigation channel and was later widened to make access from Lough Corrib to the city of Galway easier. There is evidence that weirs were constructed on many Irish rivers and that the rivers were used as important trading routes; however, little progress was made until the early eighteenth century when more serious attempts were made to carry out proper surveys and lodge plans before the Irish Parliament. In 1715, an Act was passed 'to encourage the draining and improving of the bogs and unprofitable low grounds, and for the easing and despatching the inland carriage and conveyance of goods from one part to another within this Kingdom'.

It was proposed in this Act that large numbers of rivers in all four provinces be made navigable and be linked via a series of navigable channels. Whilst the main aim of the Act was to develop the bogs and waste ground of the midlands, it was envisaged that the opening of navigable canals and rivers would improve communications throughout the country and increase the prospects for economic development.

Although some works did take place on the River Maigue near Adare, County Limerick, around 1720, little came of other projects, as finance was to be raised by Commissioners of Inland Navigation and, because of the high cost of many of the projects, little was achieved; however, it marked the beginning of the Canal Age in Ireland.

In the preamble of the 1729 Act, it was recognised that the 1715 Act had failed. It was felt that this new Act would be more beneficial because of the setting up of Commissioners of Inland Navigation for each of the four provinces, and it was to be funded by Parliament. The 1729 Act did achieve some results. In an attempt to satisfy the increasing demand for cheaper coal in Dublin, the Newry Canal was commenced in 1731 to open up access to the Tyrone coalfields, with work on an extension from Lough Neagh right into the coalfield area beginning in 1732, called the Coalisland Canal.

Newry Navigation and Ship Canal

Edward Lovett Pearce (1687–1733), the Surveyor General, began work on the Newry Canal (1731–42). However, he was busily engaged in the building of the new Parliament House in Dublin and it was his young assistant, Richard Castle, who actually took charge of the engineering works until December 1736 when Thomas Steers, a Liverpool engineer, was employed to complete the canal, assisted by a Mr Gilbert. It was a considerable engineering achievement, although imperfections were soon to be realised. It was the first summit-level canal undertaking to be completed in these islands. Extending 18½ miles, it climbed up from a tidal lock at Newry through ten locks to a summit level near Poyntzpass (78 feet above sea level) before dropping down through three locks to join the Upper Bann about 2.8 miles south of

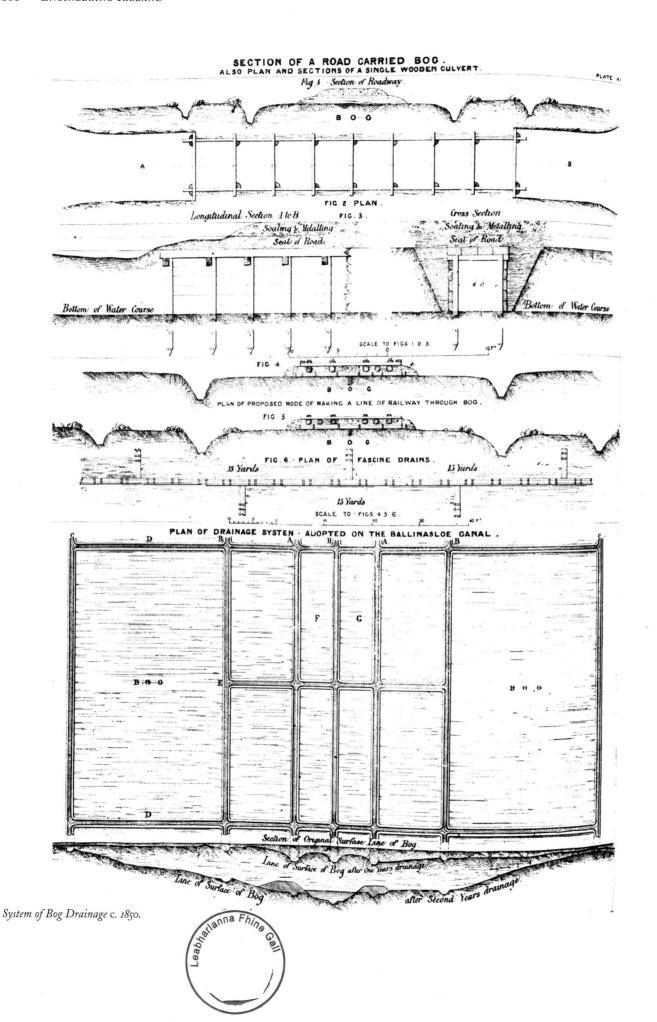

SECTION OF A ROAD CARRIED BOG.
ALSO PLAN AND SECTIONS OF A SINGLE WOODEN CULVERT.

PLATE XI

Fig 1 - Section of Roadway

BOG

FIG.2 PLAN.

Longitudinal Section A to B   FIG. 3   Cross Section
Soaling & Metalling   Soaling & Metalling
Seat of Road.   Seat of Road

Bottom of Water Course   Bottom of Water Course

SCALE TO FIGS 1 2 3

FIG 4

BOG

PLAN OF PROPOSED MODE OF MAKING A LINE OF RAILWAY THROUGH BOG.

FIG 5

BOG

FIG. 6 · PLAN OF FASCINE DRAINS.

15 Yards   15 Yards

15 Yards

SCALE TO FIGS 4 5 6.

PLAN OF DRAINAGE SYSTEM · ADOPTED ON THE BALLINASLOE CANAL.

BOG   F   G   BOG

Section of Original Surface Line of Bog.

Line of Surface of Bog after one Years drainage.

Line of Surface of Bog   after Second Years drainage.

System of Bog Drainage c. 1850.

Portadown, from where the river was navigable into Lough Neagh. The Newry Ship Canal, nearly five miles long, with a large lock at the seaward end, was constructed under the guidance of Thomas Omer between 1759 and 1769, and greatly boosted the trade of the port.

In 1751, Parliament extended the appropriation of duties for a further period of 21 years and incorporated the provincial commissioners into a single navigation board. In 1755, large sums of money were voted for public works and for the encouragement of industry. Navigation works were an obvious choice at that time, and the Commissioners of Inland Navigation, many of whom were members of parliament themselves, were able to obtain large grants for schemes.

The most important developments, which took place under the 1751 Act, were the development of the Boyne Navigation, the commencement of work on the Shannon Navigation in 1755, the Grand Canal in 1756 and the Barrow Navigation in 1759.

Boyne Navigation

Thomas Steers carried out the initial survey of the Boyne and work began in 1748 under his direction, with the assistance of his deputy, John Lowe. By the time Steers died in 1750, the tidal lock at Oldbridge had been completed. Work continued slowly until the 1760s when David Jebb took control. He had a personal interest and he completed his own mill at Slane in 1766. It had taken just under 20 years to complete the nine miles of navigation from the Oldbridge to Slane. Less than one-third was in the river and there were four stretches of canal with a total of seven locks, the last of these at Rosnaree being a double-chambered lock. One of the stretches of canal was on the north bank of the river and the others on the south bank. There were no bridges at either end of this canal to enable the towing horse to cross the river. Platforms, or 'horse-jumps' as they were called, were constructed, from which the horse stepped onto the boat he had been towing which was then pulled across the river, a difficult and hazardous operation when the river was in flood.

Some work had been carried out upstream of Slane in the 1750s by Thomas Omer but, as with so much of his work, it displayed a lack of understanding of the problems of river navigations. He used short lateral canals with narrow walls separating them from the river. These were very vulnerable to damage from winter floods, and the locks soon became ruinous, so that this part of the navigation had never been open to traffic.

In 1782 David Jebb was instructed to proceed with the works upstream of Slane but, apart from building a guard lock, or single pair of gates at the Slane Lateral Canal to prevent floodwater damaging the canal, he did not proceed any further. In 1790, Richard Evans was entrusted to continue the works upstream and was assisted by Daniel Monks and John Brownrigg. It was interesting to find so many of them working together on these early Boyne works, which turned out to be a good testing ground for future navigation works. Work continued apace and because of the many difficulties encountered, Evans decided to avoid using the river in the last 4½ miles of navigation from Stackallen to Navan, and used a single length of lateral canal instead; in 1800, the navigation to Navan was opened to traffic.

Shannon Navigation

In 1755, the Commissioners of Inland Navigation ordered their newly arrived engineer, Thomas Omer, to commence works on the Shannon, and he tackled the middle Shannon first. There were four places where the natural navigation was obstructed between Lough Derg and Lough Ree: Meelick, Banagher, Shannonbridge and Athlone. Navigation was completed to Roosky in 1769 and the Jamestown Canal finished in the early 1770s.

In the meantime, while efforts to make the Shannon navigable from Killaloe to Carrick could be said to have progressed satisfactorily, it was a very different story south of Killaloe, where enormous difficulties were encountered in the few short miles to Limerick in which the river fell 100 feet. William Ockenden, a new arrival in Ireland, was placed in charge of these works by the Commissioners. Ockenden commenced works at the Limerick end of the navigation where the Shannon makes a great loop approaching the town, but he died in 1761 and works ceased. It wasn't until the early 1780s that William Chapman (1749–1832) was consulted on how to proceed. He had established his name as engineer to the Kildare Canal Company, building the Naas Canal and then became a Consultant Engineer to the Grand Canal Company. It was not until 1799 that boats began to ply the navigation. In 1801, the Directors General of Inland Navigation sent their engineer, John Brownrigg (c. 1749–1838) to inspect the entire Shannon and produce a detailed report. Works were completed on the construction of the Errina–Plassey Canal in 1814, thus rendering the Limerick to Killaloe reach navigable. Between 1818 and 1822, the Directors built another lateral canal, the Lough Allen Canal, joining the River Shannon at Battlebridge with Lough Allen near Drumshanbo. This was completed by John Killaly (1766–1832), without doubt Ireland's most successful home-trained canal engineer.

Control of the Shannon Navigation passed to the Commissioners of Public Works on their establishment in 1831. Major improvement works, as provided for in the Shannon Act of 1839, were carried out and included the construction of locks, regulating weirs, swivel bridges and extensive channel dredging. Many of the structures are still very much in evidence today and are a testimony to the excellent craftsmanship of the period.

The building of the hydroelectric works at Ardnacrusha by the Shannon Power Development Company in the late 1920s required major alterations to the navigation. The level of Lough Derg was raised by around 2 feet, the weir and sluices at Killaloe were removed, the lands downstream of Killaloe were flooded, and the Errina–Plassey and Limerick Navigation canals were bypassed in favour of a new double lock incorporated into the power station.

Grand Canal

The Grand Canal, to link Dublin to the River Shannon, was commenced in 1756 by the Commissioners of Inland Navigation, with Thomas Omer as engineer. He was over ambitious, building locks to take 175 ton barges. Dublin Corporation, interested in canal water to supply the city, took over responsibility for construction in 1763, and Omer had been replaced by John Trail by 1768, but by 1770 less than 20 miles had been partly built and no section opened. A difference of opinion arose between Trail and Charles Vallencey, on where to cross the River Liffey, and Trail suggested that an outside expert should be called in. John Smeaton (1724–1792), who was working on the Forth and Clyde Canal in Scotland, was asked to come to Ireland to advise the company. Smeaton and his assistant, William Jessop (1745–1814), visited Ireland in June 1773. In 1777, Trail resigned and Captain Tarrant took over and, in 1779, succeeded in opening the canal as far as Sallins in County Kildare. Soon afterwards, Evans took charge and Robertstown, 7 miles west of Sallins, was reached in 1784, by which time the directors had decided that before going further towards the Shannon, they would link part of their canal by a branch to the River Barrow, then navigable at Monasterevan. Evans was dismissed in 1789, and Archibald Millar took charge of construction, with William Rhodes and James Oates as assistants. That year, with work towards Athy proceeding, the directors decided to concentrate on the 50 or so miles separating Lowtown from the Shannon, upon which nothing had been done except some preliminary drainage of the bog.

The fact that the Grand Canal in particular has large lengths of canal embankments in peat is mainly attributable

Notable early stone bridges include the four-teenth-century structures over the River Liffey at Kilcullen in County Kildare (1319) and at Leighlinbridge over the River Barrow in County Carlow (1320). Both have been much repaired and altered over time. In the sixteenth century, numbers of substantial stone bridges were erected — for example, across the Boyne at Kilcarn near Navan in County Meath and in the larger towns of Ballinasloe, Carlow and Enniscorthy. Between 1670 and 1684, four new stone bridges were erected across the River Liffey in Dublin, but all have since been rebuilt.

Leighlinbridge.

The vast majority of pre-1750 stone bridges in Ireland are likely to have been planned and built by stonemasons, but, from around 1750 onwards, most large bridges were designed, and their construction supervised, by engineers, and occasionally by architects. From then until the end of the century and into the nineteenth century, there is evidence of a Palladian influence in the design of a number of major road bridges, particularly in the more affluent areas of the southeast of the country and in Dublin.

The Parisian architect and bridge engineer, Jean-Rodolphe Perronet (1708–1794), was the first to discover that the horizontal thrust of the arches was carried through the arch spans and that the piers carry only the vertical load and the difference between the thrusts of the adjacent arch spans. By keeping the arch span the same, there would be no thrust on the piers, so the piers could be greatly reduced in thickness. In order to maintain the stability of the piers during construction, the 'centring' for all arches was erected and the arches built simultaneously, working from the piers towards the crown of the arch to minimise any thrust on the piers. The principal advantages were that the ratio of pier width to arch span could be significantly reduced, thus providing less of an obstruction to river flows, and the arch profiles could be made much flatter. Alexander Nimmo, the designer of Sarsfield Bridge at Limerick, drew his inspiration from one of Perronet's most famous bridges, the Pont Neuilly over the River Seine in Paris (opened 1772). Nimmo's bridge is now of some historical importance following the replacement of the Parisian bridge in 1956.

In the 1760s, many of the bridges spanning the Rivers Nore and Barrow in County Kilkenny were destroyed or badly damaged by severe floods. George Smith designed replacement structures under an Inland Navigation Act of 1765. He was greatly influenced by the works of Palladio and this can clearly be seen in the decorations applied to the piers and spandrels of a number of his bridges. In 1776, George Semple published his seminal *Treatise on Building in Water*, one of the classics of eighteenth-century civil engineering literature.

Only three masonry arch bridges in Ireland have single spans equal to or greater than 100 feet. A landmark in the construction of masonry arch bridges in Ireland was the bridge at Lismore, completed in 1775. It was not until 1794 that the Lismore span was exceeded in Ireland and then by only a few feet by Sarah's Bridge at Islandbridge in Dublin with a span of 104 feet 5 inches. The last of this trio, and the largest masonry arch in Ireland, is that erected in 1814 at Lucan with a span of 110 feet.

The ability to span a river with a single arch, provided suitable foundations could be found for the abutments, reduced the risk of scour and the cost of construction and maintenance. However, the increase in span with an associated

Leinster Aqueduct.

large rise in an arch, created a new problem, that of excessive gradients on the approaches to the central arch or arches. This problem was overcome in large measure by the use of flatter segmental arches.

Bridges designed in the Gothic style with pointed arches are rare, but that by Nimmo at Poulaphouca in County Wicklow (1820), and that by Killaly near Lisdoonvarna in County Clare (1824) are worthy of mention. Of similar design, Ringsend Bridge in Dublin (1812), and the Causeway Bridge at Dungarvan in County Waterford (1816) both have spandrel walls built as radial extensions of the voissoirs. The profile of the arch ring at Ringsend (like Sarsfield in Limerick) is hydraulically efficient and the masonry is continued across the bed of the river to protect the bridge against the scouring action of the river's flow.

Although small in span, canal bridges are also an important element of our inherited infrastructural heritage. In addition, a small number of aqueducts have been constructed to carry a canal over a river or some other obstruction — for example, the Leinster Aqueduct, which carries the Grand Canal over the River Liffey in County Kildare, and the Whitworth Aqueduct carrying the Royal Canal over the River Inny near Abbeyshrule in County Longford.

On the railways, substantial masonry arch viaducts carried the Dublin to Cork line over the River Barrow at Monasterevan, and the river Blackwater at Mallow, which was severely damaged during the Civil War of 1922 and reconstructed subsequently using steel-plate girders. The Monard and Kilnap viaducts near Cork, and the Craigmore Viaduct near Newry are other examples of fine masonry arch structures.

As far as the dating of Ireland's considerable inheritance of masonry road bridges is concerned, the destruction of the bulk of the Grand Jury records in the Public Record Office during the Civil War in 1922 has left a void in information relating to bridges built and, even more importantly, repaired, in Ireland during the period 1700–1898. Style can act as a guide but can rarely be relied on as sole evidence.

For many stone bridges, locally available stone or 'fieldstone' would have been used in their construction. This stone would have been naturally occurring and would have been either collected or quarried. Depending on the location, limestone, granite or sandstone would have been available, or some local geological variant of these rock types, such as 'greywacke'. Fieldstone was sometimes used in its naturally occurring state; otherwise the stone would have been dressed to fit as required. The stones would generally have been only roughly dressed. For major bridges where sufficient finance was available, good-quality stone in large blocks could be quarried, often at some considerable distance from the bridge site, or even from overseas. The stones were dressed by squaring off their faces, and these would be laid in courses. Stone, highly tooled to produce close-fitting blocks with very thin joints, is referred to as 'ashlar'.

Joints in the stonework are normally filled with *mortar*. The lime-mortar used in early stone bridges presented two difficulties — it was very slow to set and the strength could not always be relied on. The slow set made the mortar vulnerable to being washed out by flowing water or rain. To ensure good-quality quick lime, the limestone had to be raised to a sufficiently high temperature to drive off sufficient carbon dioxide, and this could not always be guaranteed. However, good-quality well-set *lime-mortar* is a strong and durable substance. When cements first became available, they were sometimes used for jointing (and in the mass in foundations) below water level, whilst lime-mortar was used above.

Possibly the most significant engineering work to affect a large proportion of multi-span stone bridges spanning the major river systems has been that of arterial drainage. Each of the main rivers and its associated catchment areas were designated as a drainage area. Much of the work carried out under arterial drainage Acts was designed to prevent or at least limit the annual flooding of lands lying adjacent to the main river channels. The channels were generally straightened and deepened and, as a result, many bridges had to be strengthened or underpinned, or replaced. It is reckoned that arterial drainage schemes have been associated with over 2,000 miles of river channel, affecting over 6,000 bridges.

Accurate methods for assessing the strength of masonry arches are of particular importance given the very large number of such structures that are still in service in Ireland. Such assessment is complicated by the wide variety of arch types and the considerable differences in their methods and quality of construction. The National Roads Authority has developed EIRSPAN, a bridge management system, and has populated a database with data from surveys of over 1,800 bridges on national roads.

Metal Bridges and Railway Viaducts

Metal bridges, generally of iron or steel, are less common in Ireland than in the industrialised areas of Britain. Primarily, this is because there was available locally stone and brick suitable for use for bridgework, whilst metal was generally more expensive or had often to be imported. The perfection of the process, whereby elements could be formed of cast iron in a mould, soon resulted in the construction of cast-iron bridges. A certain quantity of pig iron was imported and fashioned into bridge parts by small Irish foundries, and such bridges may carry the mark of the local foundry concerned. As iron foundry technology continued to advance, bridge elements were soon being cast in larger sections and, by the time of the erection of the Liffey (or Ha'penny) Bridge in Dublin (erected 1816), the six large castings forming each of the three ribs could be bolted together and cross-braced.

A major difficulty with cast iron is that, although very strong in compression, it is weak in tension. To overcome this difficulty with the material, cast-iron bridges were soon being built of two large sections cantilevered from either side and meeting at the centre or simply supporting a mid-section. The I-section solid cantilevers were deep at the abutments and these bridges generally exhibit a massive appearance. To reduce the dead weight, the webs of the cantilever beams were frequently pierced by openings and gradually the solid webs of the cantilevers were replaced with flower-like openings or by much lighter forms, such as Xs or circles, as at Oak Park in County Carlow. Apart from being strong in compression and weak in tension, cast iron has good corrosion properties but contains impurities and is quite brittle. Working the iron to drive out the impurities and to reduce the carbon content led to the production of wrought iron, and in time the production of wrought-iron I-beams.

In the early years of railway transportation, long spans presented great difficulty. One solution, developed by

Rory O'More Bridge, Dublin.

The Suir Rail Viaduct at Cahir, County Tipperary

William Fairbairn and Robert Stephenson in the mid-nineteenth century for the crossing of the Conwy River and the Menai straits in North Wales, was to form a large metal tube, or 'box girder', through which the rail traffic passed. There are no examples of this through type of large box girder in Ireland, but smaller box girders were used for the Suir Viaduct at Cahir in County Tipperary. Here, pairs of box girders were used to span between the piers and cross beams, or 'stringers', used to support the rail tracks. Within the past 25 years, there has been a resurgence of interest in box-girder design in steel or pre-stressed concrete, but with the boxes situated below rail level.

The production of wrought iron allowed the construction of large latticed girders and the fabrication of trusses, such as the Pratt truss, both capable of being used for long spans. The general arrangement was the cross bracing of these at the bottom members such that traffic passed between the side trusses. There are several examples of the use of Pratt trusses in Ireland. The main bending moment in a truss is at its mid-span and some reduction in dead weight has been achieved by using a curved top member of the truss, known as a 'bowstring truss'.

The original bridge section of the Boyne Viaduct (opened 1855) was one of the first large lattice girder bridges to be constructed using wrought iron. The viaduct consisted of 12 No. 60 foot span masonry arches on the Dublin side of the river, three wrought-iron lattice girder bridge sections spanning over the estuary of the River Boyne, the central span being 267 feet, and three similar masonry arch spans on the Dundalk side of the river. Sir John Macneill conceived the design for the bridge, the detailed design being prepared by James Barton, Chief Engineer to the railway company. The bridge section was replaced in steel in 1932.

Other major important railway viaducts include the Chetwynd Viaduct southwest of Cork, which carried the now disused Cork & Bandon Railway over the main Bandon road. It was fabricated in wrought and cast iron, has four spans of 110 feet, and was designed by Charles Nixon, a pupil of I.K. Brunel. The Kilkenny–Waterford railway line crosses the valley of the River Nore by the Thomastown Viaduct, a solid Victorian bowstring wrought-iron girder bridge of 212 foot span, completed in 1867. On the Limerick–Waterford line, the viaduct at Cahir (completed 1852) crosses the River Suir, the bridge section consisting of twin wrought-iron box girders spanning continuously over the river piers, the three spans being 52 feet, 150 feet, and 52 feet.

The line to Galway crosses the River Shannon at Athlone, the viaduct again being mainly of wrought iron. The 542-foot-long structure consists of two main spans, each 166-foot span, constructed on the bowstring and lattice principle. The bridge is supported on 12 No. 10 foot diameter cast-iron columns and there is a central swivelling opening span of 120 feet, which allowed the passage of river traffic, but is now permanently closed.

The ongoing development of Rosslare Harbour at the turn of the nineteenth century led to the construction of the Waterford–Rosslare line so that the railway could provide quick and easy access direct from Cork to London via Rosslare and Fishguard. The most significant engineering feature is the 2,131-foot long steel truss girder bridge over the River Barrow west of Campile. The bridge is the longest railway bridge in Ireland spanning entirely across water. It has 11

No. fixed spans of 148 feet each, two end spans of 144 feet, and a central opening span of 215 feet.

Between Rathdrum and Arklow, the line to Wexford traverses the valley of the Avonmore and Avoca rivers and a number of fine examples of masonry construction in granite carry the railway line over the deep gorges of the rivers. Typical of these bridges is the Rathdrum Viaduct with five masonry arch spans, each of 44 feet, and rising some 70 feet above the riverbed.

Towards the end of the nineteenth century, the railway companies in particular tended to favour the use of solid plate girders in bridges. Early plate girders were of wrought iron, but later ones were of steel when it became possible to roll sheets and sections such as angles. Plate girder bridges, although of poor aesthetic quality, tended to be cheaper, especially when replacing earlier trusses on existing abutments. They also have a robust appearance, which gave a sense of security to rail passengers. Although a number of railway bridges were rebuilt in the early twentieth century using plate girders, iron was soon displaced by concrete (apart from one or two larger bridges).

Concrete Bridges and Viaducts

Bridges have been constructed in mass or reinforced concrete since around 1900. Although such bridges tend to be utilitarian in appearance, and often lack any recognisable aesthetic qualities, they nevertheless form an important feature of transport infrastructure. Ireland possesses a range of bridge designs executed in concrete, including examples of both pre-cast and pre-stressed construction. Concrete has advantages in using local sand and stone, Irish cement and largely unskilled labour, but since the Second World War, rising labour costs have narrowed the difference in cost, and steel has once again been used on recent bridges.

Concrete has the same disadvantage as cast iron — it is strong in compression but weak in tension. Thus, initially, its use was confined to foundation work and as an infilling or 'hearting' to bridge piers and arches. Thus it was used in the Ballydehob Viaduct in west County Cork in 1886, in the Taylorstown Viaduct near Wellingtonbridge in County Wexford in 1906, as well as on the Tassagh Viaduct and some bridges of the Armagh & Castleblaney Railway through Keady in County Armagh. Subsequently, mass concrete was used in arch bridges, either built up from concrete blocks replicating stonework or cast *in situ* in one piece. The contractor Sir Robert McAlpine & Sons, in particular, promoted the use of mass concrete for bridges and viaducts, but there are only a few Irish examples.

William Wilkinson realised as early as 1854 that iron bars inserted into the concrete would make it stronger, but little was done initially to develop his ideas because of the difficulty in obtaining bars of a sufficiently consistent strength. It is generally considered that the first practical system of reinforced concrete was that developed in France by Monier (patented in 1867), which used two layers of small-diameter round bars. A number of French engineers researched further into reinforced concrete, including Lambot and Coignet, but it was the work of François Hennebique, after 1892, which was to lead to the widespread use of reinforced concrete as a construction material.

The granting of a licence by Hennebique to L.G. Mouchel in 1897 to design works in 'ferro-concrete' led to an explosion of concrete construction in Britain and, somewhat later, in Ireland. Mouchel undertook the design, while construction was entrusted to licensed contractors, such as J. & R. Thompson of Belfast. At this time, concrete often proved to be cheaper than other contemporary forms of construction.

Other designers, seeking to circumvent the various patents then in force, introduced alternative methods of reinforcement, often working on a design-and-build basis. There was considerable debate over whether the use of a large

'The Deeps' Bridge at Killurin in County Wexford.

number of small-diameter bars was preferable to concentrated reinforcement, such as the Moss rail-type bars used on Hartley Bridge, spanning the River Shannon to the north of Carrick-on-Shannon. There was also debate as to whether pre-formed mesh, such as that used by the British Reinforced Concrete Company (BRC) in the bridge spanning the River Slaney at Killurin in County Wexford, or the punched and expanded metal sheets of the Expanded Metal Co., were preferable to individual bars.

Resistance to shear was provided in ferro-concrete construction by flat bar stirrups, although round bar stirrups later became the norm in reinforced concrete. Kahn bars, with a diamond section having attached fins acting as shear reinforcement, were used in the King's Bridge in Belfast around 1910. Many early bridges did not have the amount of shear reinforcement now considered essential and a number have been strengthened as traffic loadings have increased.

The bond achieved between the reinforcement and the concrete was another matter of some concern. Insufficient bond would allow the bars to pull out under load. Some designers used ribbed bars, such as those used on the Boa Island and Roscor viaducts in County Fermanagh by the Indented Bar and Engineering Company, or various forms of twisted bar to improve the bond. Current practice is to continue the bar for a predetermined distance past the point of zero stress or to form a hook on the end of a straight bar.

Pre-casting is the term used when sections or elements of a structure are cast away from the site and brought to the site for erection. Pre-casting allows work to be undertaken under much more even and controllable conditions. An obvious first form of pre-casting was the manufacture of concrete blocks, sometimes referred to as cast-stone. These may be employed in the same way as stone or brick in arch bridges. There are, however, surprisingly few examples in Ireland of this option. Bridges having pre-cast deck beams or pre-cast columns or balustrades are more commonplace. One of the first bridges to employ large pre-cast elements was the footbridge to the Mizen Head fog signal station in County Cork, erected in 1909. Here, the arch was made up from U-shaped trough sections, which, once in place, were filled with concrete.

As concrete is weak in tension, the carrying load on a beam may be increased if it is first put into compression. This is the underlying principle of pre-stressing, with the first practical experiments being undertaken on the European mainland in the 1930s. Wires, usually called tendons, are placed and then stretched before being anchored against the end of the beam. Release of the stressing-jack then introduces compression in the beam. Pre-stressed beams may be either pre- or post-tensioned. Pre-tensioning is useful for small beams, and for items such as fence posts or guardrails, and was the system first used. The wires are stretched on a frame in the casting yard and the beams are cast around them. A continuous bond thus exists between the concrete and the tendon. First used in 1952 in a road bridge replacement over the main rail line near Sallins in County Kildare, and, shortly thereafter, in a bridge at Mount Norris in County Armagh, pre-tensioned beams are now widely used.

The alternative method, and that needed for large beams, is to cast the beam first, leaving ducts for the tendons. These are then threaded in and stressed after the beam has attained its design strength. There is now no continuous bond with the concrete. At first, attempts were made to fill the duct with cement grout but the effectiveness of this procedure is debatable. The viaduct near Dee Street on the Sydenham Bypass in Belfast was built in 1959, but concerns over water ingress and possible rusting of the tendons led to its demolition in 1998. Large-span modern bridges are now frequently made up of a number of segments strung together in the manner of pearls on a necklace. The joints between each segment are glued using special epoxy resins, the beams subsequently being post-tensioned.

Kenmare Bridge in County Kerry.

Most concrete bridges have a flat-deck profile, either with pre-cast beams or cast *in situ* slabs, with or without attached beams. The flat profile is occasionally relieved by incorporating a drop-down to the support. Arch bridges tend to look more pleasing and some good examples exist with open spandrels to the arch. In the 1930s, a number of bridges with a bowstring profile were built, that at Kenmare in county Kerry being an example.

Large motorway interchanges, which incorporate several individual concrete bridges, appeared in Ireland with the opening of the first section of the M1 south of Belfast in 1962. The bridges on the early sections are of solid appearance with solid slab piers. As confidence in the use of concrete has grown amongst designers, the appearance of concrete bridges has become lighter, with continuous beams and solid piers being replaced by open V-sections or rows of columns.

Balanced segmental construction has been used for large motorway bridges. This construction technique involves sections of cast concrete being erected alternately to either side of a support such that the out-of-balance force on the support is never more than that due to one segment. Match casting allows for more efficient jointing between the segments. During match casting, a segment is formed in the casting yard and allowed to harden. Its neighbour is then cast against the end, thus ensuring a perfect fit. The first section is next taken and placed in the bridge, the second segment is moved across and its neighbour is cast up against it. This continues until one half of the structure has reached a little short of mid-span. When the corresponding half has been erected from the adjacent support, the two are formed into one continuous span by means of an *in situ* concrete 'stitch'.

Although concrete as a construction material is not without its problems, its cost effectiveness and ability to span large gaps will ensure that it continues to be used for many bridge structures in the foreseeable future.

Recent Developments

Since the 1980s, there has been a significant development of Ireland's infrastructure, much of it resulting from an upsurge in economic activity and the provision of European Union and state funding. This process received a boost with the founding in 1993 of the National Roads Authority (NRA) and the Railway Procurement Agency (RPA) in 2002. New road building, road improvements and the upgrading of the rail infrastructure have resulted in the rehabilitation or replacement of many bridges on existing routes, and the erection of numbers of new bridges on, under or over motorways, bypasses and other parts of the improved transportation infrastructure. In particular, the upgrading of that section of Euroroute I in Ireland linking the port of Larne in County Antrim with Rosslare Europort in County Wexford by way of Belfast and Dublin, has contributed to a large increase in bridge-construction activity. The provision of new river crossings has resulted in a variety of design solutions and construction techniques being used in Ireland, many for the first time.

Bypasses have been provided to remove heavy through-traffic from congested town centres and road alignments improved by the removal of sharp bends, often the result of the reluctance of early bridge-builders to construct bridges on a skew. Significant investment has continued to be made in strengthening existing bridges to accommodate the heavier axle loads of commercial traffic now permitted by the European Commission.

The upgrading of much of the railway infrastructure is continuing. A major consequence has been the replacement of many of the stone-arch over-bridges with structures having a more rectilinear profile to improve clearance for high-speed train movements and the refurbishment, strengthening or total replacement of bridge structures at some river crossings.

The various basic bridge designs have been in use for many years and, following the introduction of the technique of pre-stressing of concrete in the 1950s, major advances in bridge design have, until recently, been few, although span lengths have tended to increase. Modern designers have the advantage of a better understanding of the properties of materials, better quality control of materials and the benefit of computers, which can now analyse more complex structures. Recent trends in bridge construction have been towards a greater use of pre-cast elements. These can be manufactured more accurately with better quality control off-site. Recent bridge projects have generally favoured segmental concrete construction (such as the West Link Toll Bridge in Dublin and the Cross Harbour Bridges in Belfast), but there have also been some examples built in steel (for example, the Foyle and Wexford bridges)

Research into the efficient design of pre-cast concrete beams has resulted in the design of a range of standard types and their more frequent use. For example, a system of pre-cast arch sections, 2.5m wide, for carrying roads over railways (or canals) on a marked skew, has been developed. In 1999, the NRA formally adopted the UK Highway Agency's *Design Manual for Roads and Bridges.*

An awareness of the impact on the visual environment of bridges is growing and recent constructions have seen a marked improvement in bridge aesthetics. For example, considerable improvement in the appearance of concrete work can result from the use of pre-cast facing panels or special formwork to mould the concrete. Improvements have come partly from more contracts being awarded on a design-and-build basis in open competition. Increasingly, such works are being undertaken on a total-package basis, with the project being carried out from conception to completion by the competition winner (often a consortium of companies). On the one hand, this process may serve to drive down the cost; on the other, it may provide an impetus for more innovative design, as has been evidenced by some recent bridge designs, such as the Millennium and James Joyce bridges, and the proposed Guild Street–Macken Street bridge over the River Liffey in Dublin.

The concept of a cable-stayed bridge is not new, but a recent upsurge in their use has resulted mainly from the fact that they offer the opportunity of crossing large obstacles with elegance and economy. However, this type of design is equally suitable for small and medium-span structures, which tend to be far more numerous. The reasons that can lead to the choice of a cable-stayed solution are many, but one of the principal advantages is the clearance available below the deck; the difference in the layouts of the cable-stays is one of the fundamental and distinguishing elements. The use of composite steel/concrete decks allows for a considerable reduction in the dead weight of such structures and in a simplification of their method of erection.

James Joyce Bridge in Dublin.

Although bridges do not represent the bulk of the expenditure on new road works, they do have a high visual impact on the public who use these transportation facilities. Motorway over-bridges are frequently of a standard design, but attempts are now usually made to vary the detailing of piers and abutments to good effect, or to use the arch form to produce a more aesthetically pleasing structure, provided that a suitable foundation is available. Structural engineers and architects therefore put considerable effort into producing bridge designs that are both structurally sound and visually acceptable.

The pace of development is increasing. Between 1997 and 2002, about 200 bridges were added to the NRA's stock; from 2003 to 2010, it is expected that around 500 additional bridges will be constructed in the Republic. There is also considerable growth in Northern Ireland and many new bridges have recently been completed.

9

DOCKS AND HARBOURS

Ronald Cox

Timber Wharves

The earliest form of facility for vessels discharging cargo at coastal settlements consisted merely of wooden poles erected on the banks of river estuaries to which vessels could be moored and their cargoes transferred from ship to shore or vice versa. Earthen banks and timber wharves or jetties evolved from Viking times, when the Scandinavians made Dublin the major port of northwest Europe and Limerick another great trading centre. The Normans valued ports as sources of revenue and established timber quays and other facilities for landing goods and persons at such places as Waterford, Youghal, Wexford, Limerick and Derry.

Timber piles driven into the river or seabed supported a braced timber deck, a technique used from early times. As the draught of vessels increased, so successive structures (embankments, timber revetments, timber and masonry walls) were advanced further into deeper water. Gradually timber wharves and jetties were replaced by longer-lasting masonry quays and piers.

Stone Quays

The first stone-faced quays appeared at Dublin along the River Liffey, along the Abbey River at Limerick, and at Wexford and Waterford. Stone quays were frequently combined with timber landing stages to enable vessels to remain afloat at all stages of the tidal cycle, rather than 'take the ground' at low tide. Piers were also built to shelter vessels and allow for the transfer of goods and passengers.

During the mid-nineteenth century, deep-water quays were provided at many Irish ports to meet the demands of an increasing overseas trade. The building of masonry quay walls was normally carried out below tide level behind temporary timber cofferdams, pumps being employed to counteract leakage. When berths needed to be deepened, the older quays usually required underpinning, again involving costly temporary works. For example, between 1870 and 1912, 8,326 feet of quays along the River Liffey in Dublin was replaced with new masonry quay walls on mass-concrete foundations, following completion of which, Dublin could describe itself as a deep-water port.

Fishery Piers and Harbours

In the later years of the eighteenth century, there was some improvement to fishing harbours, such as the building of the innermost pier at Dún Laoghaire. Civil engineers, such as Alexander Nimmo and John Killaly, were commissioned to survey and report on the piers and harbours needed to develop a fishing industry, particularly along the western seaboard. Commissioners were appointed in 1819 to grant money for the erection of piers. Their powers were transferred in 1830 to the Board of Inland Navigation and then to the Board of Public Works (OPW). In 1842, Commissioners were appointed to improve and regulate Irish fisheries, and £40,000 was granted for work on fishing piers and harbours. Several smaller harbours were developed by local landowners in order to encourage fishing and other trade, particularly the export of grain and import of coal — for example, at Courtown in County Wexford and at Carnlough in County Antrim. Major marine works were undertaken along the western seaboard between 1891 and 1914 under the Congested Districts Board, particularly stone piers and small harbours in support of an expanding fishing industry.

The Department for Communications, Marine and Natural Resources has statutory responsibility for the harbours at Killybegs, Rossaveal, Castletownbere, Dunmore East and Howth. The harbours at Ardglass and Donaghadee come under the Department of Agriculture and Rural Development, which is responsible for the fishing industry in Northern Ireland. Several other harbours have been developed for the fishing industry, notably at Kilmore Quay in County Wexford and Kilkeel in County Down.

Harbours

A harbour is a body of water deep enough to provide anchorage for ships. So-called 'harbours of refuge' are either natural, such as Cork, or artificial, such as Dún Laoghaire. Artificial or 'asylum' harbours consist of one or more break-waters or piers located in such a manner as to protect shipping riding at anchor or berthed within the harbour from the effect of stormy conditions. This was particularly important in the days of sailing ships, as many were lost from being driven onto a lee shore, a particularly frequent occurrence along the eastern seaboard during easterly gales. The design and construction of harbours constitutes one of the most challenging branches of civil engineering.

The problem with the approaches to Dublin and other ports situated on river estuaries along the east coast of Ireland, such as Drogheda, Dundalk, Wexford and Belfast, was that the rivers flowed over strands at low water and formed natural, but constantly shifting channels. Prior to the nineteenth century, it was generally thought that building out into the river, thereby narrowing the channel, would increase the depth of water available to vessels wishing to berth in the port. Although this approach did help to define a navigation

Dunmore East Harbour, County Waterford.

channel, depths were generally not improved until the introduction of mechanised dredging in the mid-nineteenth century. In addition to the problem of the depth of water available in such ports, accumulations of sand and silt formed a 'bar' at harbour mouths. In some cases, the problem was exacerbated by the construction of piers or moles in the wrong locations, causing sand to be deposited across the entrance channel.

In the case of Dublin, as far back as 1711, work had commenced on the provision of a straight channel from the city. A jetty was first formed of timber caissons, floated down river and sunk in position by filling them with rubble. By 1796, the so-called South Bull Wall (one of the longest sea walls in Europe), designed to prevent movement of sand from the south strand (or 'bull'), had been completed using twin-masonry walls in-filled with sand. Following a series of surveys of the bay, Francis Giles (1788–1847) and George Halpin (Snr) (c. 1775–1854) provided an ingenious solution, in 1819, for naturally deepening the channel across the 'bar' at the entrance to the port. Having studied the tidal cycles in the bay, they decided to construct a wall or breakwater from the north shore to a point opposite the end of the South Bull Wall and separated from the shore by a channel spanned by a timber bridge. As the engineers were not sure what the effect of their proposal would be, they built the first 5,500-foot section of the wall to full height, a length of 1,500 feet to high water neap tides, and the remaining 500-foot section to half-tide level. The effect of this chance, but nevertheless remarkable, piece of harbour engineering (completed 1825) was to cause natural scouring of the entrance channel to the port. During the first half of the ebb tide, both the tidal and river waters confined within the North and South Bull walls pass partly over the submerged portion of the North Bull Wall, and partly through the harbour entrance between the walls. The result is a great increase in the velocity of the current and the removal by scouring action of sand from the bar at a time when the ebb tide is setting eastwards towards deep water. Because of the direction of the currents on the north side of the bay, the flood tide from the south does not normally return sand to the harbour. Over a period of some 40 years, the depth over the bar at low-water ordinary spring tides had increased by 10 feet and opened up the port of Dublin to deep-water vessels. As Sir John Purser Griffith later remarked, this was 'a noble example of directing the great sources of power in nature for the use and convenience of man'.

Mail (Packet) Services

Meanwhile, insufficient depth of water at Pigeon House Harbour and a general shortage of berths in Dublin port had been causing such delays to the mails from London that, from 1800, various proposals were put forward, including an alternative harbour to be constructed at Howth on the north side of Dublin Bay. Work commenced in 1807 and continued under the direction of John Rennie (1761–1821). The harbour was completed in 1826 by his resident engineer, John Aird (fl. 1782–1832). Howth was formally established as the mail packet station in 1818 when a lighthouse was added at the end of the East Pier. Because of difficulties of access, the harbour was a failure as far as the mail-packet vessels were concerned and the service was transferred in 1826 to Dún Laoghaire. In fact, Rennie had originally advocated Dún Laoghaire as a more suitable harbour, but work at Howth had already commenced when he took over.

In 1815, harbour commissioners were appointed to arrange for the building of a new 'asylum' harbour at Dún Laoghaire. The initial design consisted of a single 2,800-foot long pier, but in 1817, John Rennie was consulted and proposed two embracing piers, later known as the East and West piers. Following the death of Rennie (Snr) in 1821, his son, John (later Sir John) Rennie, took over as consultant and proposed two short projecting arms from the ends of the piers, leaving a narrow entrance. The final form and length of the pier heads was delayed until the Board of Public Works took over the work in 1833. The outcome was to form an entrance to the harbour of about 760 feet with rounded pier heads. A lighthouse and various wharves and piers were provided later within the harbour to accommodate the mail ships operating from Holyhead.

In the late eighteenth century, Donaghadee on the coast of County Down was chosen by the British Post Office as a port of call for the mail packet ships from Portpatrick in Scotland, and some rebuilding was undertaken between 1775 and 1785. A new harbour was designed by John Rennie, and construction supervised by his son John between 1821 and 1836. The 900-foot long south pier has four arms or 'kants', the slightly shorter south pier being separated from the shore by a shallow channel. Like at Howth, the packet vessels had difficulty using the harbour in adverse weather conditions, and the service was transferred to Larne in 1867. Here, harbour works had been commenced in 1845, and a rail connection with Belfast completed in 1862. The Rennies also completed harbours at Portrush and at Ardglass, where the first breakwater was destroyed in 1838 and was not rebuilt until the late 1870s.

The Post Office selected Dunmore East at the entrance to Waterford Harbour for the location of a harbour for the mail packets operating from Milford Haven in South Wales The original 780-foot long pier and lighthouse were built between 1823 and 1825 to the design of Alexander Nimmo. A substantial parapet wall provides shelter from easterly gales, the seaward side of which is protected by battered masonry slopes or pavement. Considerable additions were made in the 1960s and 1970s during the development of the harbour as a major fishery port, and further extensions are currently being planned.

In 1873, two long timber jetties were provided at Rosslare Harbour at the southeast corner of County Wexford to provide berths for passenger steamers from Fishguard in South Wales. Following the extension of the railway from Wexford, a new jetty reached by a viaduct was provided. A new harbour was constructed between 1904 and 1906, including a 1,550-foot long jetty. The harbour was completely rebuilt, firstly in the 1960s and again in the 1990s and is now a major ferry terminal and container port.

Wet Docks

Wet docks may be totally enclosed by quay walls with entrance locks to maintain a minimum depth of water at the berths at all states of the tide, as at Limerick, or may be in the form of a tidal basin with deep-water berths dredged to a minimum depth at ordinary low tide, as at the Alexandra Basin in Dublin.

In Dublin, a wet dock had been opened by the Grand Canal Company at Ringsend in 1796, together with three sea locks and three small dry docks. The Custom House Dock, George's and Inner docks had previously been completed on the north bank of the river under the direction of John Rennie. By the mid-1850s, there was a significant increase in activity because of the improvement of conditions at the 'bar', and the general increase in world trade.

Most of the masonry quays along both sides of the river were rebuilt between 1850 and 1910 in the traditional manner. However, for the deep-water extension,

Wet Dock at Limerick.

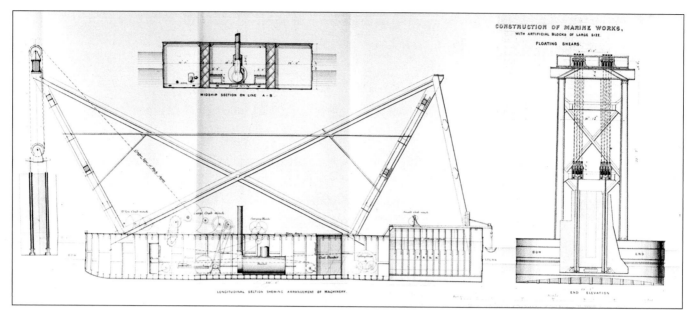

Concrete block-laying float (c. 1870).

Bindon Blood Stoney (1828–1909), Chief Engineer of Dublin Port, pioneered a different method of creating quay walls. He constructed large monolithic mass concrete blocks on land and placed them in position using a massive floating crane. Each block was placed on a levelled foundation prepared by labourers working under compressed air from within a diving bell. Using this method, the first length of the North Wall Extension was completed by 1885, the remainder being completed in the 1930s using reinforced concrete floating caissons.

In Belfast, development of the port had also been hampered by lack of depth, until William Dargan cut the first access channel in 1840. Dredging has always been associated with the maintenance of deep-water access to ports, bucket- or suction-dredgers being used, depending on the nature of the dredged material. Dredged spoil, when suitable, has usually been used for land reclamation, as at Belfast, where the spoil from the Dargan (Victoria) Channel was used to create Queen's Island on which were to be located the ship-building activities that made the city famous.

Dry Docks

The building and repair of ships necessitated either slipways for smaller vessels or graving (dry) docks of ever-increasing size. The first graving dock at Dublin (1860) was soon exceeded in length by the Hamilton Dock at Belfast (1867) and by that at Limerick (1873). The development of Belfast as a major centre for ship-building (Workman Clark and Harland & Wolff) led to the construction of a series of large dry docks, the Alexandra (1889) and Thompson (1911), used by such ocean liners as the *Olympic* and *Titanic*. Later, the 1,150-foot long Belfast Dry Dock (1968) and the vast Building Dock (1970) accommodated large tankers and bulk carriers up to 338,000 dead-weight tons.

Other Docks and Harbours

The quays along the River Lee at *Cork* are approached along a dredged channel from Lough Mahon, an arm of the large natural harbour formed between the headlands at Roches Point. The largest ocean liners were able to anchor in the

This was in turn subject to the evolving technologies of the steam turbine, the marine diesel and later gas turbine/water jet propulsion.

The single hull configuration of boat/ship design, which has long existed, has in recent years given way to multi-hull catamaran and trimaran (SWATH designs — small waterplane, twin hull) for fast-ferry designs such as the Irish Ferries *Jonathan Swift* or Stena Line's HSS, SeaCat and SeaLynx-type fast ferries.

This ongoing development of ship design has meant that ports

High Speed Ship (HSS).

have continually had to update existing configurations and construct new facilities and modern terminals to provide an adequate service to accommodate these new concepts and faster ships. This has meant the provision of longer and deeper berths, bigger and heavier capacity cranes, and ever more sophisticated and higher capacity roll on/roll off double-deck ramps and modern passenger terminal facilities. These developments have allowed faster vessel turnaround time and have also included the provision of more land for cargo marshalling and storage.

The main features of the evolution and growth of ports and the engineering contribution to their development include facilities, such as specialised equipment, shipbuilding/repair, storage, features, cranes, bridge ramps, transit/storage, sheds, oil tanks and grain silos. This may best be exemplified by noting the developments at Dublin Port during the twentieth century.

Dublin Port

As the nineteenth century was coming to a close, the first oil tanker, the *Potomac*, arrived and discharged to storage tanks. In 1902, an electricity generating station (DC supply) was built on the cross-berth near East Wall Road, this development signalling the modernisation of the port under the then Chief Engineer, Sir John Purser Griffith (1848–1938). Similar modernisations and developments were to continue throughout the twentieth century. Three years later, ten 4-ton capacity cranes and one of 100-ton lifting capacity were erected on the North Quay Extension, the latter remaining in service until being dismantled in 1987.

By 1913, the first reinforced concrete grain silo had been erected, although there were somewhat earlier examples, such as those at Sligo and Waterford. Construction of Alexandra Quay commenced in 1921 using reinforced concrete cellular caissons designed by Purser Griffith's successor, Joseph Mallagh. This method of construction was used until the 1980s for quay berth construction, Berth No. 49 in Ferryport being the last such construction. There was considerable building activity following the Second World War, including the erection of the four-storey Stack 'D' tea warehouse, which provided around six acres of covered storage. This was closely followed by the construction of the first Ro/Ro Bridge Ramp on Ocean Pier, this time using pre-stressed concrete deck beams. Nearly 100 years after the completion of the No. 1 Graving Dock, the No. 2 Graving Dock, with steel floating caisson-type gates, was opened in 1957.

The 1960s saw the start of the 'container revolution', with the installation of dedicated cranes of 30-ton capacity and 30-ton and 40-ton capacity transporter ship-to-shore container cranes in the various port terminals. Over 200 acres of land was reclaimed from the sea for terminals to cater for container handling and also oil/chemicals storage facilities. There was also growth in the Ro/Ro mode of transport.

Following the introduction by B&I Line in 1979 of the first high-speed cross-channel service on the Dublin–Liverpool route, using a 'Jetfoil' craft, the *Cú na Mara*, the next two decades witnessed the demolition of most of the old and redundant transit sheds and cranes and the construction of new passenger terminal facilities and marshalling areas for cars and freight. 'Fast ferries' (i.e. speed in excess of 40 knots) and large capacity 'Super Ferries' (30 to 50,000 ton DWT, compared to previous generation of ferries of around 4,000 ton DWT), placed ever-increasing demands on the port authority. To meet capacity demands, the first double-deck Ro/Ro bridge ramp in Ferryport was installed in 1995.

Towards the end of the last century, the container berths at Ferryport and at South Bank Quay were deepened,

Dublin port.

steel sheet-piling being driven in front of the caisson quay walls, anchored back, the depth on the berths thereby being increased by 4m.

Port of Belfast

In 1847, the Belfast Harbour Act repealed previous acts and led to the formation of the Belfast Harbour Commissioners. This new body, with much wider powers, completed the second stage of a new approach channel to the port and from that time the Commissioners have developed and improved the port, reclaiming land to accommodate new quays, new trades and changes in shipping and cargo-handling technology. The efficient, modern port of today is evidence of the foresight and commitment of successive generations of Harbour Commissioners.

The Port of Belfast is the principal maritime gateway serving the Northern Ireland economy and increasingly that of the Republic of Ireland. It is a major centre of industry and commerce and has become established as the focus of logistics activity for Northern Ireland. Around two-thirds of Northern Ireland's sea-borne trade, and a quarter of that for Ireland as a whole, is handled at the port, which receives over 9,000 vessels each year.

With almost two million passengers and half a million freight units annually, Belfast is Ireland's busiest ferry port. It is also Ireland's leading dry bulk port, dominating the market with regard to imports of grain and animal feeds, coal, fertilisers and cement, and exports of scrap and aggregates. Over 95 per cent of Northern Ireland's petroleum and oil products are also handled at the port.

Engineers of many disciplines continue to play a crucial role in the design, construction and maintenance of the complex port facilities required to handle today's sophisticated cargoes.

Irish Shipping Limited

The main Irish ports all gave birth to shipping companies, but one that should be mentioned specifically is Irish Shipping Limited. The company was set up by the Government of the neutral Irish Free State in 1941, during the dark days of the Second World War. It provided an essential lifeline for the supply of food and fuel. Great bravery was shown by the crews who sailed during this critical period in old and often inadequate ships, and 149 crew members were lost in attacks and sinkings during the 'Emergency'. In the post-war period, the company's fleet was replaced with new vessels, culminating in 1981 with the construction of a 'Panamax' class bulk carrier of 71,500 tons DWT, the *Irish Spruce*, built in the Verolme Dockyard in Cork. In 1984, severe financial difficulties overwhelmed the company, which was rapidly put into liquidation by the Government, all the praise for past services rendered to the state being quickly forgotten. It could be said that Irish Shipping fell victim to 'market forces' driven by the ever-increasing competition for lower maritime transport costs provided by low-paid Third World crews and the transfer of vessel registration to 'flags of convenience' states.

Shipbuilding

Belfast

The illustrious history of shipbuilding and design in Belfast is described later in the chapter on the engineering industries of Northern Ireland and will not require repetition here; suffice to record that prior to the founding of Harland &

Wolff in 1862, boat and shipbuilding was carried on in Belfast from the mid-seventeenth century onwards. The building of iron ships, from 1853, laid the foundations for the later success of Harland & Wolff and, from 1880, when their engine works for the manufacture of propulsion machinery commenced production, it can truly be said that they were a world-class shipbuilder.

Dublin

In 1790, a vessel of 500 tons was launched in Dublin, the largest to be built in Ireland up to that time. Iron and steel shipbuilding in Dublin dates from 1864, the yard of Messrs Walpole, Webb and Bewley being located adjacent to No. 1 Graving Dock (opened 1860). The business of shipbuilding and ship repair was carried out by a succession of companies, such as the Dublin Dockyard (1901–1922), taken over by Vickers (Ireland) and becoming the Liffey Dockyard in 1940. Several ships were built for the B&I Steamship Company prior to the completion of the liner tender *Cill Airne,* built 1962 for Cork Port. The yard ceased trading in 1981.

Although shipbuilding is now a distant memory, ship repair continues, particularly in No. 2 Graving Dock (opened 1957). There were two graving slips adjacent to the dockyard — No. 1 Slip (dating from 1830) was used for the repair of smaller craft (work boats, tugs and pilot cutters); No. 2 Slip was for larger vessels (1,100 tons), and was equipped with a powerful winch for pulling the vessel and cradle up the slipway slope on guide rails, for repair. These two slips are now gone with the land and water nearby reclaimed for use and incorporation into the North Quay Extension Ro/Ro terminal.

Cork

During the first half of the nineteenth century, the Cork shipyards were the most extensive in Ireland. In 1828, Cork, along with Dublin and Waterford, was one of the first Irish ports to have a dockyard equipped with a patent slip. In the era when Cork Harbour was an important base for the Royal Navy, Rushbrooke was the site for a graving dock (designed by Sir John Rennie and opened in 1857) and a ship-repair establishment. In 1959, this repair yard was taken over and modernised by Verolme United Shipyards of Rotterdam, employing approximately 1,000 men at its peak. The yard was equipped with a dry dock, two floating docks and two slipways and was equipped to build and launch ships in excess of 50,000 tons DWT, including several bulk carriers for Irish Shipping Ltd.

The yard also constructed Ro/Ro ramps, accommodation modules for offshore platforms, submersible pontoons and many structures and ship fenders of various types. Sadly, as a result of Far East competition, the yard closed down in the 1980s.

Waterford

The nineteenth-century shipbuilding ventures of the Quakers in Waterford, in particular the Malcomsons, were as technologically advanced as any similar development of the day. Their iron shipyard was ahead of Belfast and was the leading Irish centre of iron shipbuilding between 1846 and 1861, employing in excess of 400 workers. The yard was early in emulating Brunel's ship-design features, including the provision of watertight compartments in the construction of ship hulls. Many steamships/liners for the North Atlantic (for example the S.S. *Iowa* of 1,781 tons for the London–Le Havre–New York service, launched in 1863) and the cross-channel trades were built in the Neptune yard, particularly in the period after the Crimean War. The last vessel to be built at the yard was the steam yacht, *Maritana,* in 1882.

11

IRISH MARITIME LIGHTS

Gordon Millington

THE EARLIEST ATTEMPTS AT MAKING SEA NAVIGATION SAFER at night were the work of the people who cared for the life of their fellow human beings — the ecclesiastical orders. It seems most likely that the first-established maritime light in Britain and Ireland was a fire established at Hook Head at the entrance to Waterford Harbour and the navigable rivers Suir and Barrow, probably about AD 470. At that time, little was known about the production of light and how to make it visible over a long distance or how to make one light distinguishable from another, a licence for the wreckers to establish bogus lights to lead ships aground so that they could plunder them. The next light is believed to have been at Youghal, established in 1190 and in the care of the nuns at St Ann's convent. The upkeep of this was funded by an endowment from Maurice Fitzgerald. It thus seems probable that the lights were mainly of use in good weather, and ships stood off the coast in bad weather. The tower that stands at Hook Head today was started in 1245 and was built by the warden and chaplains of the monastery of St Reneuan. There were no laws requiring these lights to be kept working, and they were frequently out of commission

In 1665, King Charles II's parliament granted a franchise to Sir Robert Reading (member of Parliament for Ratoath). This required him to establish six lights around Ireland, two at Howth, two at Kinsale, one at Hook Head and one at Magee Island (the entrance to Larne Lough,) and he was required to provide a surety of £5,000. In return for building and maintaining the lights, he was allowed to collect dues of a penny per ton from all inward and outward-bound ships. Ships from foreign ports generally paid two pence per ton. Even the lights established by this scheme, which was the only licence issued for Ireland, were not properly maintained. The principle of dues to be paid by the user for the provision and maintenance of navigation aids was thus established and, some 340 years on, is still used to fund the service. It seems that there was an attempt with some of the fires to reduce the amount of smoke, and so prevent it from obscuring the light, the first evidence of some scientific thought and engineering being applied to the lights.

Hook Head lighthouse.

Over the next 140 years, few additional lighthouses were established, but there were advances in scientific knowledge. The use of Argand oil lights seems to have begun about 1780. This was a very important advance, allowing better control over, and a better quality of, light and was much more powerful than the tallow candles that had replaced fires, whether wood, turf or coal were used to fuel them. Gaslights appeared about 1814, with an ingenious system of using a black rod which, when heated by the sun, would reduce the supply of gas as the sun rose. A more sophisticated version is still used today to control the supply of gas to the mantle.

The change of use of lighthouses from location indicators in good weather to an aid to navigation in bad weather is evidenced by the dissatisfaction with some lights, particularly by merchants who wanted their goods delivered on time and without danger of their loss at sea. Some lights had been placed so high that they were either shrouded in clouds or hidden by fog when they were most needed. By 1791, chronometers had become the means of accurate navigation, following the developments by John Harrison and the lever escapement developed by Thomas Mudge. This allowed ships out of sight of land to obtain a good positional fix from the stars and the sun. Thus total reliance on 'dead reckoning' was no longer the primary means of navigation, although accurate timepieces also enabled 'dead reckoning' to be much more accurate. All this meant that ships could, without having visual contact, approach closer to the shore than before. But sight of the shore was still needed at close quarters, so there was an increased need for lights and buoys.

In 1789, Thomas Rogers (d. 1812), a glasscutter who had joined in business with George Robinson, an optical expert, was responsible for the installation at Howth Head of a silvered glass reflector behind large plano-convex lenses. This so impressed the authorities in Ireland that Rogers broke his connection with Robinson and settled in Ireland in 1792. He was then involved in the improvement of more lights and was responsible for the building of several lighthouses and altering the system of light from candle to oil in others. His only surviving structure is on the South Rock off the County Down coast, which was to be built of granite blocks dressed in Wexford. The ships chartered to carry the blocks to the site never made it, one sinking and the other ending up in Penzance. Mourne granite stones were then sourced locally. This was the first wave-washed rock on the Irish Coast to have a lighthouse. Smeaton's Eddystone had already been built but was superseded in 1882 by a new structure by James Douglass (1826–1898). Robert Stevenson's Bell Rock was not completed until 1811. So, the South Rock structure is the oldest surviving wave-washed lighthouse and only the second to be constructed around the coasts of Britain and Ireland. The light was known as the Kilwarlin Light and is reckoned to be one of the great examples of lighthouse engineering. It had been built inside some other offshore shallows that continued to take their toll on shipping and it was abandoned in 1877, being replaced by a lightship. The South Rock (Kilwarlin) tower is still a useful day mark for small boats sailing the inshore passage.

Rogers was also responsible for the construction of the lights at Cranfield and Aranmore. His other great contribution to navigation was the design of the light itself. It was the first revolving light and gave a white flash from ten oil lamps with two-inch diameter wicks and ten silvered reflectors of 15-inch diameter. The frame was kept in motion by weights. Fifty years later, there were still only eight revolving lighthouses around the coast of Ireland and Great Britain.

The ability to have lights with different characteristics was important. For example, in 1906, the captain of the *Hazeldene*, being unaware of a change that had occurred to the character of a light just a few weeks earlier, became confused and ran his ship ashore. A similar fate befell Captain Hoskin, the master of the *Great Britain*, Brunel's famous ship. He was on passage from Liverpool to America and passing up the County Down coast at night. He saw a light that he assumed to be on the Scottish coast, so he ordered it to be left to starboard. It was St John's Point, a light installed by George Halpin Snr and first lit in 1844. However, by 1846, Hoskin had still not marked it on the chart he was using, so the *Great Britain* ran aground in Dundrum Bay. A similar incident happened in 1977 when a ship going north mistook the South Rock Lightship for Killintringan Lighthouse, which had the same light characters, and so ran aground at Kearney point. The South Rock was then changed from a red to a white light.

Rogers, despite his success in developing the science of lighthouses, was later heavily criticised for his inability to control the cost of the work of both the construction and maintenance of the lights in his care. The period was marked by a lack of effective management of the various lighthouse bodies and their performance. Various attempts to make the control and management of navigation marks more workable and reliable had not been successful. The Lighthouses (Ireland) Act 1810, passed after several scandals, made the Port of Dublin Authority, better known as the Ballast Board, responsible for the maintaining and commissioning of lighthouses around Ireland. They appointed Halpin Snr to the post of Inspector of Lighthouses. He had, since 1800, been in the employment of the Corporation for Preserving and Improving the Port of Dublin, as Chief Engineer, a post he continued to hold.

This change of control, and the appointment of a man with proven engineering and management ability, seems to have enabled a step change in the provision of lighthouses along the coast of Ireland. Halpin remained in his post for 47 years. He built around himself a team of very capable engineers and seems to have consulted widely with other capable professionals. This group of engineers perfected the art of building structures able to resist the violent forces imposed on the structure by the might of the sea and wind. They also left for us to admire, at least in calm weather, towers with great aesthetic appeal, an appeal that has not dimmed in the passing years. During this period, 37 lighthouses were constructed, mostly new, but some rebuilds. Not all were a success, such as those made of cast iron — for example, the first tower on the Fastnet Rock.

Among the works attributed to Halpin is the Tuskar Rock light. The Tuskar Rock, if any sea is running, is awash at high water, so building the foundations was difficult. Work started in 1812 with the establishment on the rock of a wooden dormitory to house the men during periods of reasonable weather. However, during the night of 18 October, waves wrecked their dormitory, ten men being swept into the sea and fourteen surviving to tell the tale. Such were the dangers that were accepted in those days as part of everyday life. The tower is a bell-shaped structure of granite. The light revolved with two white and one red flash and, interestingly, Robinson, Rogers' one-time business partner, supplied the light.

Dunmore East lighthouse.

Dundalk Bay Pile light.

It was Halpin who recognised the remarkable work of Alexander Mitchell, born in Dublin, but brought up and educated in Belfast. By the age of 21, he was totally blind. For 30 years he ran a very successful brick-manufacturing business in Belfast. He had, however, a natural aptitude for maths and science and his interests included mechanical experiments. In 1830, he designed a screw mooring that he developed into a screw pile for use as a foundation in soft ground. Between 1842 and 1851, four lighthouses were built on structures designed by him. One quite unique lighthouse, also acting as a pilot station, was on the Holywood Bank in Belfast Lough, but is now dismantled. The other examples in Ireland are in Dundalk Bay, on Spit Bank in Cork Harbour and near Dungannon in Waterford Harbour. His only real failure was an attempt to drive piles into the Kish Bank. They failed in the first winter storm before any superstructure was constructed.

Most lighthouses, including those by Halpin, were constructed on land, although often in remote locations, such as the lights on the Skelligs, on Eagle Island and the two on the Maidens. Because of their remoteness they need very good logistical management and that must have been one of Halpin's strongest points as he achieved so much during his period of leadership. George Halpin Jnr, who had worked under his father, took over from him and remained in the post until 1864. He continued with the good work and was responsible for some nine new lighthouses, including the exposed light on Rockabill.

Halpin Snr's last great project was the design and construction of a light for the most exposed and dangerously sited rock around the coast, the Fastnet Rock. For this he chose cast iron supplied by J. & R. Mallet, the Dublin iron founders. The tower was over 63 feet high and was tapered from 19 feet to 13 feet 6 inches. Constructed of flanged panels, the lower three feet was filled with rubble masonry and the wall up to the first floor was lined with masonry 3 feet 6 inches thick. The light was 148 feet above sea level. Halpin died in 1854, just after construction was complete, so it was examined by the Consulting Engineer to the Corporation, Charles P. Cotton, and by George Stevenson of the Northern Lights Board. Seas could reach a height of 133 feet above sea level in bad conditions and the tower would tremble during storms, so it was strengthened in 1867. In 1881, winds of 80 knots hit the area of the Fastnet Rock. The tower of the nearby Calf Rock was broken off just above the masonry strengthening at the base; no one was injured. This structure, also by Halpin, was to a similar design as the tower on the Fastnet, which suffered damage to its light in the same storm. So the long-term durability of this form of construction was questioned. As the science of the production of the light beam had improved, the importance of this light to transatlantic traffic called for a modern powerful beam. These two factors led to the decision to build a new tower on the Fatsnet Rock.

William Douglass had taken over as Engineer-in-Chief of Irish Lights in 1878; he was responsible for the design of the present Cornish granite tower on the Fastnet. Work commenced in 1896 and much of the credit for the construction of what is one of the finest lighthouses in the world must go to the charismatic foreman from Wicklow, James Kavanagh. C.W. Scott, who had taken over from Douglass, designed the optical apparatus and the lantern, manufactured by Messrs Chance of Birmingham. The light was supplied by new paraffin-vapour incandescent burners, with the lens floating on a bed of mercury, and was lit for the first time on 27 June 1904. Lights had now reached a power where the

Sunderland Flying Boats moored near the Harland & Wolff shipyards in Belfast.

Aircraft Manufacture

The northeast of Ireland, with its strong history and traditions of mechanical manufacturing engineering, inevitably attracted aviation industry to the area. Short Brothers, originally based in the southeast of England, established an aircraft-manufacturing facility near Belfast early in the 1900s and eventually transferred all its activities there in 1936. Between the world wars, Short Brothers was to the fore in developing the 'flying boats' that served as the first commercial passenger-carrying long-haul aircraft. During the Second World War, the company continued to manufacture the Sunderland 'flying boats' that operated regularly between North America and a newly constructed base at Foynes on the Shannon Estuary.

Short Brothers also manufactured a large number of military aircraft, mainly bombers, during this period, and was taken over temporarily by the British government in March 1943. In the post-war period, Short Brothers entered the evolving civil aviation industry with the manufacture of aircraft such as the Canberra, Skyvan and Belfast Freighter. With the advent of 'wide-bodied' aircraft in the 1970s, and the much tougher competition from the larger manufacturers, the company became involved in component manufacture of wings, nacelles, and advanced lightweight composites. The short-haul SD 330 and SD 360 were introduced during this period, and Shorts sold a number of the SD 360 aircraft to Aer Lingus when the airline set up its commuter subsidiary. Arising out of that deal, Shorts contracted with Aer Lingus to be the primary carrier of all Shorts-manufactured aircraft components to Boeing in Seattle, an interesting example of North–South commercial cooperation. The manufacturing facility near Belfast has an airport on-site that was subsequently adapted to accommodate short-haul European flights.

Shorts 360, manufactured in Belfast.

Founding of Aer Lingus

The momentum towards the development of land-based, commercial air services to and from Ireland gathered pace rapidly during 1935. Several proposals were made to the Free State Government, but these were rejected, mainly because of proposed foreign ownership without any state involvement. However, in 1933, a Scottish operator, Midland and Scottish, opened a route from Glasgow to Belfast (Aldergrove), which operated successfully for a number of years. Civil aviation became the responsibility of the Department of Industry and Commerce and, in May 1936, aviation telecommunications became a separate division of the Department of Posts and Telegraphs, and a new radio station (Dublin AERADIO) was set up at Baldonnel. In the same month, Aer Lingus Teoranta was formally incorporated 'To carry on and foster the pursuit of aviation in all its forms both within and without Seorstát Éireann'. On 27 May 1936, a De Havilland 'Dragon', carrying five passengers, took off from Baldonnel for Bristol. At the time, there were wide-ranging views in Government as to the strategic and economic justification for a national airline, but Minister Sean Lemass and Department Secretary John Leydon had the pragmatic vision to push the plan through. It was regarded as essential for the sovereignty of the state to have an independent airline.

In late 1939, despite the outbreak of war in Europe, flights continued to operate to Britain, and passenger numbers gradually increased. In December 1939, the airline purchased a Douglas DC3 aircraft and, in January 1940, the first flight operated from the new Dublin Airport at Collinstown in north County Dublin. The site was also, like Baldonnel,

Part III

Construction and Public Works

& Bailey were leading ironwork fabricators, for example erecting the wrought-iron rail viaduct over the River Nore at Thomastown, south of Kilkenny.

The commercial process of making wrought iron from cast iron had been developed in the eighteenth century and it was widely produced and used in structures. Wrought iron was costly to produce compared with cast iron, the final stage being the so-called puddling process, which was based on heating the iron to a pasty consistency in a puddling furnace and working it manually to expose it to a hot-air blast, this being followed by repeated rolling. Despite this, the product had much more satisfactory tensile properties and was capable of being forged and bent, resulting in its use as a structural material for much of the nineteenth century, until it was displaced by cheaper mild steel.

It was known that good steel could be produced from Swedish ores, which were low in impurities, and the possibility of making steel from commercially produced pig iron was obviously attractive, especially if it could be produced more cheaply than wrought iron. In Britain, Henry Bessemer developed the Bessemer converter in 1857. In the converter, pig iron was heated to a temperature well above its melting point, and hot air was blown through the molten mass to control the carbon content of the fluid metal, depending on whether iron or steel was required. The refractory lining of the converter had a significant effect on the quality of the finished product. Bessemer's process was, in a short time, made obsolescent by the development in 1863–65 of the Siemens-Martin open-hearth process for steel-making. Although slower, it was even cheaper to operate because of reduced difficulties with the refractory lining and the more efficient use of heat. Despite this, Bessemer plants were set up all over Europe and both methods of producing steel were widely used.

Before Bessemer's revolution, steel had been produced by processes similar to the puddling process used to produce wrought iron. Wrought iron remained the preferred structural material because it was regarded at the time as having more consistent properties. Steel was widely criticised as an unreliable material, and doubts were expressed as to its suitability for structural engineering. The matter of the reliability of the materials was of prime importance, as well as the differentiation between the two materials for both structural and mechanical use.

The steel industry came late to Ireland. In 1938, David Frame (1876–1946), a leading scrap iron merchant, set up Irish Steel Ltd on the site of a former British naval dockyard on Haulbowline Island in Cork Harbour. The rolling of merchant steel from imported scrap material commenced in August 1939, nearly a century after the closure of the Belfast ironworks that had been using native ore and coal in the production of iron plates for shipbuilding. The first steel bar to be produced in Ireland emerged from Irish Steel's rolling mill just prior to the outbreak of the Second World War. It then became impossible to procure the materials and equipment necessary to make the Haulbowline plant a viable proposition — for example, the installation of a furnace to produce its own steel billets for the rolling operations. Under these difficult conditions, the company was forced into receivership in April 1941. With government assistance, the company struggled on during the 'Emergency', during which some 8,000 tons of steel were produced until, in 1947, the company was taken over by the Government and an open-hearth furnace installed to allow at last the production of steel from native scrap, a development supported by the Government in the *First Programme for Economic Expansion*. Hammond Lane Foundry in Dublin was the principal supplier of scrap iron to Irish Steel.

By the early 1960s, Irish Steel had become of vital importance to a rapidly expanding construction industry, supplying basic steel reinforcement in the form of round bars, flats and angles, both to the home market and markets abroad as far away as New Zealand. Irish reinforcement steel was even used in the UK in the construction of early motorway bridges and viaducts.

In 1966, a bridge to the island from the mainland was opened and, in 1973, an electric-arc furnace was commissioned at the Haulbowline works. Following the discovery of large quantities of natural gas off the Cork coast, it was suggested that the gas be used to heat the furnaces, but government policy at that time was to use the gas for electricity and fertiliser production. During 1975, there was a worldwide collapse in the steel market and a temporary suspension of steel production.

In 1979, following an agreement with a French steel producer with the support of the then EEC, a major expansion of the plant at Irish Steel was undertaken and the future for a while looked bright. However, the last two decades of the twentieth century were marked by increasing competition from large steelworks abroad and, in 1995, the undertaking was sold by the government to Ispat International, an Indian-based conglomerate, which formed Irish Ispat Ltd to run the plant. However, continuing market and production difficulties forced the company into liquidation in 2001, and the plant was closed.

Structural Concrete

The substantive history in Ireland of the material known today as concrete began in about 1850. Some 900 years earlier, during the tenth century, lime-mortar was introduced in Irish building. It is clear from surviving ecclesiastical structures and other secular buildings of the period that the bedding mortar used did, on occasion, perhaps fortuitously, possess certain of the characteristics of modern concrete.

In 1673, Sir Bernard De Gomme, preparing his estimate for a citadel to be built near Dublin included for '2000 bushells of tarras [trass] to be used in the building of walls in the front to the seaside'. This is possibly the first of very few references in Irish history to the use of a pozzolanic element similar to that used in the earliest Roman concrete in the enhancement of the traditional lime-based mortar used in Ireland.

One hundred years further on, in 1756, John Smeaton, in rebuilding the Eddystone lighthouse, designed and used a bedding mortar, based on a hydraulic lime from the argillaceous limestone of Somerset and Italian pozzolana. This man-made equivalent of the ancient Roman concrete represented a reintroduction into building of a material largely lost for over a thousand years. Possibly from this beginning, there flowed a period of research and commercial ventures into various cementitous mixtures, primarily of calcium and silica. A minor player in the field was Bryan Higgins of Sligo, who patented a variety of cement in 1779 and in 1780 published in London a book on its nature.

This frenetic period of research and innovation in several countries may be said to culminate with the patenting by Joseph Aspdin, a Leeds mason, on 21 October 1824, of 'An improvement in the modes of producing an artificial stone', which he named as Portland cement. This cement and the concrete made with it have steadily improved to become today the chief material of construction throughout the developed world. The arrival of structural Portland cement concrete in Ireland was low-key. The primary building materials here had been stone, brick and timber; and many significant buildings had foundations of lime-based concrete of one kind or another.

Period 1850–1900

In 1878, Robert Manning, then President of the Institution of Civil Engineers of Ireland, recorded, 'I was I believe one of the first engineers who used (Portland Cement) in Ireland in the tideway of the river Glyde in the year 1850', and added that in the 1870s he had 'used it exclusively, and in large quantities in marine works with every promise of complete success'. There was at this time much concern about the fire resistance of buildings. Concrete was seen as fire resistant and was used to protect iron floor and roof structures against fire. This combination of iron (itself a new structural material) and concrete gave rise to many patented 'systems' of slab construction, each with its own characteristics. One of these, the Fox and Barrett System, patented in 1844, was used by Francis Fowke in the new National Gallery of Ireland in 1857–58. This may have been the earliest use of a patented system in Ireland, and possibly the first structural use of Portland cement in Irish building. The next 20 years saw some significant advances.

Firstly, the compressive strength of concrete was recognised. The iron compression flanges in the systems were eliminated, the metal henceforward resisting the tension and the fire-resistant concrete resisting the compression. This led to the use of small discrete rail sections and later to square and round rods as tensile reinforcement.

Secondly, mass concrete walls began to replace stone and brick masonry.

Thirdly, reinforced concrete as we know it today came quietly into the public eye and asserted its position in the years 1877 to 1879. This was through the experimentation of the American, Thaddeus Hyatt, the pioneering works of the Frenchman, Joseph Monier, and the steady and practical applications of one of the foremost systems organisers, François Hennebique. These years may be seen as marking the beginning of modern reinforced concrete.

Fourthly, the most significant advance for Irish concrete between 1860 and 1880 was the work of Bindon Blood Stoney (1828–1909), who was Chief Engineer at the Port of Dublin from 1862 to 1898. His studies of Portland cement, and in particular his pioneering use of 350-ton pre-cast concrete blocks in the construction of quay walls at the port underwrote the status of this material in Irish building. It is fitting to recognise him as the 'father of Irish concrete'.

The growing use of concrete in Ireland led to the establishment of Irish cement manufacturers. In 1881, the Cooper family built cement works at Drinagh near Wexford. This was followed by the Irish Portland Cement and Brick Company in Dublin in about 1887. Both companies appear to have ceased production by about 1924. Towards the end of the nineteenth century, most structural concrete was reinforced, much of it with light I-sections of various profiles set at quite large spacing, a useful feature in estimating the age of our early reinforced concrete constructions.

Period 1900–1925

A new era for concrete began at the opening of the twentieth century. In 1887, the first book on reinforced concrete design was published in Berlin. Within 20 years, Christophe had reached the second edition of his textbook on the subject, listing in its bibliography over 300 items from eleven countries. In 1905, Marsh listed 43 systems from eight countries, then in use. At this time, the control of reinforced concrete was almost entirely in the hands of system specialists, each with an individual approach to design, and sometimes a chosen list of franchised contractors. Twelvetrees, in his text of 1907 on concrete-steel building, describes 35 buildings, and offers a select list of some 420 structures in Britain and Ireland, including 22 in Ireland. An advertisement in this book records that the Yorkshire Hennebique Contracting Company had completed no fewer than 11,000 Hennebique structures by that time.

Virtually no statutory control regulations existed in 1900. By about 1914, however, most western European countries and many cities had the forerunners of the present codes and regulations in service. The finest example of bridge design of this period, and arguably the most daring reinforced concrete structure ever built in Ireland is the Mizen Head footbridge at Mizen Head in County Cork, completed in 1909. Other Irish buildings of this period, all probably system-based, included the main river bridge and a granary at Waterford, brewery works in Cork, an elevated reservoir and linen factory in Belfast, a bonded warehouse and printing works in Dublin, a five-storey mill complex in Sligo and a bridge in Kilkenny.

Probably influenced by the promulgation of codes and regulations, there was a move in Ireland at this time towards practice-based design that did not rely on a system. The influence of the systems would, however, persist in Ireland for a further 50 years.

During the early years of structural concrete, there was controversy about the compaction of concrete and its appropriate water content. For many decades, prevailing opinion favoured the use of sufficient water to ensure nominally 100 per cent compaction. Vibration was not used and plasticizers were not known. Attention to mix design was minimal. In Chicago in 1918, however, Abrams published his findings on mix

Mizen Head Footbridge, County Cork.

design. His first principle was that 'with given concrete materials and conditions of test, the quantity of mixing water determines the strength of the concrete so long as the mix is of workable plasticity'. This principle of the water/cement ratio has governed mix design ever since. In Ireland, H.N. Walsh's seminal book in 1939, entitled *How to Make Good Concrete*, strongly influenced Irish practice.

Irish concrete came of age with the construction of the Shannon Scheme, completed in 1929. It was the first great project of the new state and in its construction used 43,000 tons of cement in 170,000cu.m of concrete. It is safe to say that concrete was the only medium with which these works, particularly the generating complex at Ardnacrusha, could have been built.

Period 1925–1945

The short period from the foundation of the Irish Free State to the outbreak of the Second World War saw a steady stream of building for a range of functions, with concrete being widely used. This period that began with the Shannon Scheme was dominated at its conclusion by the first stages of another major hydroelectric programme based on the Liffey above and below Pollaphuca and including a number of new concrete bridges.

The organisation of each project, large or small, tended, as in most countries, to reflect the sophistication of its specification and its observance on site. Hand tamping of the concrete was quite normal at this time and vibration rarely used. The importance of the water/cement ratio was acknowledged, but its subordination by the concreting gang in the interests of easier compaction, was not unknown. Off-site-mixed concrete was not available at this time. Arbitrary volume batching was usual, whereas weigh batching was quite rare. The water content of aggregate and the attendant bulking were understood, but frequently ignored. The control of cement quality could be difficult because of uncertainty of origin. On the other hand, the demands made on concrete by the codes then current were less stringent than those of today. Twenty-eight-day cube strengths of 16N per mm² and 21N per mm² were specified for ordinary reinforced concrete and more heavily stressed sections respectively. Specified covers could be as small as 18mm and 25mm for secondary and main reinforcements respectively. The net effects of these pros and cons generally provided good working structures, sometimes significantly stronger than necessary, although corrosion always remained a threat, and the concept of carbonation was virtually unknown. Most of these weaknesses were avoided on well-organised sites,

A recent trend in water-tower construction has been to use smoother wineglass-shaped designs, that at Kiltrough near Drogheda being a typical example. The provision of such towers was boosted by the introduction into Ireland of an Austrian simplified shuttering system, first used for towers at Rathlee and Dromore West in County Sligo.

Pipes and Pipelines

The earliest pipes were of lead, or bored elm or fir logs, and suitable only for low pressures. Wooden pipes were used in Dublin, Cork and Belfast up to the early years of the nineteenth century. Although iron-casting technology was capable of producing large artefacts as early as 1500, iron pipes for water supply came into use only after the invention of the spigot and socket joint in 1785. They rapidly replaced wooden pipes in the period 1810–1820. The first iron pipes were cast in short lengths and were usually of 7½-inch bore, and laid in parallel where greater capacity was needed, but, with the introduction of the vertical casting process, larger diameters and jointing variations became available. Spun-cast pipes, lighter and of more regular dimensions became available in 1922 and ductile iron pipes were introduced about 1975. Unlined iron pipes are subject to incrustation by oxidation products with serious loss of carrying capacity.

The technique of lining and sheathing steel pipes with bitumen was developed in the 1920s and made these an attractive alternative for large-diameter pipelines. They can be manufactured with a wall thickness to suit any desired pressure and had many advantages in use over the older cast-iron pipes. Ductile iron pipes with mortar lining have many of the advantages of steel and are currently more cost-effective in water and sewer applications.

Asbestos-Cement (AC) pipes were introduced in 1928 and have been popular in the size range 100–500mm. They do not corrode internally like iron pipes and so retain their hydraulic performance, but are rather fragile. Because of the health risks associated with asbestos and the cessation of local manufacture, AC pipes are no longer used in Ireland. About 1960, plastic pipes in PVC were introduced and competed with AC for use in rural pipelines. Polyethylene pipe has proved very serviceable and replaced the more expensive copper for service connections.

Pre-stressed concrete pipes made using the Rocla process were first used in the Lough Neagh supply for Belfast, and subsequently have been used for many large pipelines in Ireland. These can be made in sizes up to 1,800mm.

Water Treatment

Slow-sand filters, first used in the Vartry supply for Dublin in 1867 have been widely used in other works throughout Ireland, with major installations at Lough Neagh in recent years. Disinfection by chlorine was first practised in Reading in 1904 and was soon adopted in Ireland on the larger installations, and is now universally used. Physico-chemical treatment was introduced in the 1920s, and is essential for treating turbid and coloured waters. In this process, coagulant chemicals are used to precipitate colloidal solids and colour in settlement tanks. The water is then filtered to remove remaining fine debris and the filtrate then disinfected. Developments in this treatment process have resulted in much enhanced efficiency in clarification and filtration, and the application of electronics has provided closer process control.

Ozone is an extremely powerful oxidant and can be used both to remove colour and for disinfection, usually after micro-straining to remove any visible suspended matter. The Lough Gill treatment works in Sligo, for example, uses this process.

The Republic of Ireland is unique in making the fluoridation of water supplies a statutory requirement for the improvement of dental health, but fluoridation has been rejected in Northern Ireland by a large majority of the District Councils.

The chlorination of waters, which contain organic colour, leads to the formation of trihalomethanes, which are carcinogenic, and these are now the cause of some concern. Slow-sand filters do not remove colloidal colour and the trend will be to replace installations of this type by physico-chemical plant.

Local Influences on Water Supply in Ireland

Demography and Climate

The Republic of Ireland has a low population density, a high proportion of the population being located in coastal cities and towns. The ten largest towns are all on the coast and have an aggregate population of 1.5 million or 40 per cent of the total. The largest inland town has only 20,000 persons and the six largest inland towns together have only 92,000 persons. Of the total population of 3.6 million, 58 per cent live in towns.

The overall population density is 55 persons/km², compared with 234 for Germany and 107 for France, but when the coastal population is excluded, the population density of the inland area is only 33 persons/km². This low population density results in a correspondingly low pollution loading on water-supply resources, and in comparison with the UK and Europe, our surface waters are usable for water supply without resorting to complex multi-stage treatment processes. The rural population is more widely dispersed in single dwellings than anywhere else in Europe, making the provision of piped water expensive. Dairy farming is widely practised and generates a significant demand for water. The demography of Northern Ireland is broadly similar.

The influences of climate characteristics on water supply in Ireland are: frequent rainfall and low evaporation ensure that river flows have high minimum values and the reliable yield of catchments is relatively high; continuous groundwater recharge ensures that aquifer yields remain near constant; special measures to protect treatment plant, mains and services against frost damage are not required; and water demand for lawn watering, gardening, and other domestic activities is generally low.

Geology and Landform

More than half of Ireland is underlain by carboniferous limestone. Igneous and metamorphic rock is present in large areas of Donegal, Connemara, south Leinster and around Carlingford Lough. A wedge of Silurian rocks stretches from the east coast to the centre, under Down, Armagh, Monaghan, Cavan, and Louth. Old Red Sandstone predominates in the Southwest, Tipperary, Kilkenny and Waterford. Generally, these rocks are covered by glacial deposits or peat accumulations of varying thickness. Igneous and metamorphic rock is impermeable and useless for groundwater supply. The value of limestone as an aquifer depends on the degree of fissuring. Water from it is clear and palatable but very hard and sometimes has high levels of sulphur, iron and manganese compounds. The risk of pollution from surface sources is considerable. Ireland has few high-yielding aquifers comparable to those in England but modest yields, sufficient for local needs, can sometimes be found in buried gravels and the sandstone districts. Overall, only 20 per cent of the national supply is derived from groundwater, probably the lowest percentage in Europe, excluding Norway.

Ireland's central plain and coastal mountains give rise to large, slow-flowing river systems, some of which, such as the Shannon, Erne and Bann with large lakes, act as natural reservoirs. The southern half of the country, Counties Clare and Kerry excepted, has few lakes, and the larger water supplies are based on direct abstraction from rivers or from impoundments in some cases, as at Cork and Waterford. The proximity to Dublin and Belfast of elevated catchment areas makes a gravity supply possible for most of the water supplied to these large centres.

constructed in mass concrete using travelling steel formwork. From its terminus at Rathcoole, the supply continued to a break-pressure tank at Saggart and thence in a 33-inch-diameter steel pipe to a 19Mg service reservoir at Tallaght. A 27-inch-diameter steel pipe brought the supply from Tallaght to the city.

In recent years, this system has been developed in a number of stages towards an ultimate capacity of 340 Ml/day with additional water over and above the Corporation's entitlement being purchased from the ESB on a quantum basis. A 1,600mm pre-stressed concrete pipe, 25km in length was laid to operate in tandem with the aqueduct between the treatment plant and the break-pressure tank at Saggart and major new trunk mains laid from Saggart to Tallaght and onwards to and through the city to the northeast suburbs.

The Liffey supply also serves central Kildare, including Naas and Newbridge, and the Tallaght and Lucan–Clondalkin 'new towns'. For the latter, a new service reservoir, capacity 100Ml was constructed at Belgard and new trunk and dis-

The dam at Poulaphouca, County Wicklow.

The overflow bellmouth at the North Reservoir at Roundwood.

tribution mains laid as the towns developed. This reservoir is of unconventional design using a flexible membrane in the floor and earthen embankment and an articulated roof to cope with blast vibration from the nearby quarry.

The North Dublin Supply

Dublin County Council commenced work on a scheme in 1965 aimed at the provision of piped water to the entire area of the county north of the Liffey. A draw-off had been incorporated in the ESB hydro dam at Leixlip during construction, and abstraction rights purchased from the Board. A physico-chemical treatment works was constructed close to the dam, with six centrifugal pumps to deliver the filtered water through 675mm steel rising main to a 23Ml service reservoir at Ballycoolen. A trunk main was laid northwards, with branches serving the Airport, Swords, Malahide, Skerries, Balbriggan and all of the villages and rural area of Fingal. The 'new town' of Blanchardstown is served by trunk mains laid from Ballycoolen reservoir, and water is also supplied to the north city through a number of inputs on its northern boundary. The treatment plant has been increased in capacity in three further stages to a current output of 175Ml/d. This increased output required a second rising main, a new pumping station and increased storage at Ballycoolen. A new 70Ml service reservoir has been constructed with the unusual feature of mass concrete walls.

extensive and complex, and services can now account for more than half of total building costs in some building types. The architectural historian, Reyner Banham, wrote, 'a building is modern in so far as its plan and sections are adapted to the mechanical control of the environment.'

Development

The origins of services are firstly in mining, later in industry and in brewing, and in Ireland the shipbuilding centres of Belfast, Waterford and Cork. An account of the services provided for the *Titanic* (built in Belfast 1910–12) would indicate that the engineering of accommodation as well as propulsion in shipbuilding was well ahead of building engineering, with extensive mechanical ventilation by variable-speed fan motors, comprehensive electric installations and lighting, push- button lifts, and sophisticated telephone and emergency installations. The continuity of design and construction of a series of magnificent ships over many decades was not to be matched in the building industry of the time.

The manufacturing industry, requiring controlled conditions and access to water and waste disposal, brought about both the need for and the means of improvement. Components for manufacturing were then adapted for use in large residential and institutional buildings. Comfort and convenience became achievable where affordable. Existing buildings were fitted out as best they could be. New buildings were to some extent designed to accommodate services, although architectural values even still neglect the special needs of services.

Prior to the Second World War, services were mostly indicated by architects rather than specified, and were designed and specified by specialist contractors. Consulting engineers were few. Office of Public Works and Department of Health engineers were involved on public buildings and hospitals. By the mid-1930s, services form a significant element in building programmes. Soon indigenous firms came gradually to supplant the British firms.

Fuel and Energy

In pre-railway mid-nineteenth-century Ireland, imported coal was the main fuel used in the port cities. Elsewhere, the fuel was timber and peat, primarily for cooking, incidentally for heating. Later, rail and barge brought coal to inland towns. Petrol-generated gas was introduced, to be followed later by coal gas in urban centres. The 1938–43 'Emergency' saw the return of turf for urban fuelling, even for Dublin households, with families harvesting their own fuel in the Dublin and Wicklow Mountains. A magazine and burner, the so-called Mona Jet, was widely used, and turf-burning was government policy for public buildings even into the 1950s. Oil then became more generally used, light grade for smaller plants, cheaper heavy grade for larger plants. Coal gas, and later natural gas, replaced oil for domestic and commercial plants.

Public gas supply, initially for street lighting, was used later for the lighting of buildings and for cooking and water heating, and was used in some public spaces for induced flued ventilation. Coal gas was limited to major towns. There was much criticism of gas and burner quality in the early years, and of a monopoly of supply in Dublin. Elsewhere, industry, institutions and major houses relied on in-house gas-generating plant.

From the early 1880s, electricity gradually replaced gas, Carlow being the first to adopt electric street lighting (1889). Electricity also replaced belt-driven power. Natural gas replaced coal gas in Dublin and elsewhere from 1976. Alternative energy sources as yet have little application but may well become significant. Ireland has a very energetic wind climate and solar energy is available all year for water and pool heating. Tidal energy has great potential.

Central Bus Station and offices (Busaras) in Dublin.

Off-peak electricity became and has remained a feature, especially for home space and water heating. Some notable 1960s major off-peak electricity space-heating installations were at Holles Street Hospital and Kildare Street government offices, both in Dublin, the former still in use.

Lighting

Natural day-lighting proved inadequate for deep commercial buildings. So-called artificial lighting became a requirement not only in hours of darkness, but also to supplement daylight and enable suitable internal work areas.

Pre-industrial lighting was by candle and paraffin, continuing in many buildings well into the nineteenth century. From the 1850s, gas lighting appeared, first for street lighting, then for buildings, but not effectively until improved mantle design in the 1870s. By the 1880s, electricity proved better and safer for lighting, and later cheaper, but competition continued.

Electric lamp developments, from very limited arc to incandescent and discharge sources, allowed a great range of quality, lamp life and efficiency. The fluorescent lamp has become the building lamp enabling general room lighting to the high levels now expected and has displaced the previous use of low-level general lighting augmented by local task or desk lamps. An early use in Dublin was at Busaras (the central bus station) in the 1950s.

Sanitation and Fire Fighting

It is difficult now to imagine the unsanitary conditions of urban living even into the twentieth century, without running water or waste-disposal facilities. Domestically, the local hand pump, the bowl, the hipbath, the bedroom 'po', the earth closet or the street dump served. Offices, shops and places of assemby fared little better.

on its ability to industrialise. Irish mill-wrights and engineers played a crucial role in the adoption and development of new water-powered prime movers, whilst Irish industrialists demonstrated alacrity in their efforts to maximise the resources nature had placed at their disposal, rarely matched by their English contemporaries. Even in the nineteenth century, steam power in many Irish industries was a supplement rather than a replacement for water-powered prime movers. In 1870, water power accounted for almost a quarter of Ireland's recorded industrial horsepower of 9,879hp, with the Irish textile industry being responsible for just over 83 per cent of the Irish total water power.

To date, an incomparable corpus of early water-powered mill sites in Ireland has been scientifically dated, either by dendrochronology (tree-ring dating) or radiocarbon dating, to the period from the early seventh century to the thirteenth century. There are, indeed, more dated pre-tenth-century water-powered mill sites in County Cork alone than there are in the rest of Europe. The vast majority of these watermills, as both the documentary and archaeological sources

Windmill at Blennerville, County Kerry.

clearly indicate, were horizontal-wheeled mills. In the horizontal-wheeled mill, the waterwheel has a vertical driveshaft and the waterwheel rotates in a horizontal plane.

Changes in water levels affected by the tides around Ireland's coastline were also exploited by watermills from at least the seventh century onwards. Through the use of millponds filled by the incoming tides, tide mills had a regular, seasonally uninterrupted source of water, with which a mill could be operated during the ebb tide. The entire process was then repeated, the pond being filled on the rising tide. The world's earliest recorded tide mills, dated by dendrochronology to about 617, have recently been excavated at Nendrum on Strangford Lough, whilst two further watermills at Little Island, County Cork have been dendro-dated to around 630. Tide mills are also known to have been used at Basra on the Persian Gulf in the tenth century, but elsewhere documentary references to their use in Europe are somewhat later. The horizontal-wheeled mill survived in Counties Down and Sligo up until about the end of the seventeenth century and in Counties Galway, Mayo and Roscommon up to the present century.

The use of the vertical waterwheel in Ireland is at least as early as the horizontal waterwheel. The vertical waterwheel, as it name suggests, rotates in the vertical plane on a horizontal axle. But unlike the horizontal waterwheel, the motion of its axle cannot be directly transferred to the mechanism it is to set in motion. Some form of intermediate power transmission (in early mills usually gear wheels set at right angles to each other) was always necessary. One of the most basic types, the undershot waterwheel, in which the water strikes the waterwheel near the lower part of its circumference, had been employed at Little Island, County Cork, around 630.

Up until the second half of the eighteenth century, all Irish waterwheels were made entirely of wood and were, invariably, mechanically inefficient. However, by the 1770s, some Irish foundries were already manufacturing cast-iron waterwheel axles for export, and it seems reasonable to assume that some of these were being used in Ireland around this time. In the early 1800s, Thomas C. Hewes (1768–1832) of Manchester was developing what was to become known as the suspension waterwheel. Before the introduction of this type of waterwheel, the motion of the wheel was transmitted to the gear wheels via its wooden axle. In the suspension waterwheel, however, power transmission from the wheel was transmitted from its rim. Heavy wooden axles could now be replaced with slender cast-iron ones, with internal wrought-iron suspension rods providing support for the framework of the wheel. In about 1802, Hewes erected the earliest-known Irish example of a suspension waterwheel at Overton Cotton Mills, near Bandon, County Cork. This was 40 feet in diameter and 5 feet wide and, while most of it was made of metal, the soleing and the buckets were of wood. On present evidence, this would appear to be the first example of such a waterwheel ever built, and fortunately its original shaft has been retained *in situ*.

The development of the water turbine presented enormous opportunities for many Irish industrialists, particularly those involved in branches of linen manufacture. Here was an excellent opportunity both to capitalise on existing water resources and to reduce an increasing reliance on steam-powered plant. Irish industrialists and millwrights were, for the most part, quick to grasp the significance of this new technology. On an island with limited coal resources, the continued development of existing sources of water power became a technological imperative for Irish industrialists. The water turbine offered considerable advantages over the various existing types of vertical waterwheel. By the late 1840s, water turbines could produce efficiencies equal to and often higher than the most developed vertical waterwheels, utilising falls of less than one foot up to hundreds of feet. The equivalent range for vertical waterwheels was about 2–50 feet and, whereas the vertical waterwheel could not operate efficiently when flooded, the water turbine could continue to work effectively when entirely submerged. The earliest-known turbine operating on the reaction principle, in Ireland, was at work at Brague in County Down in 1834. This appears to have been a type of Barker's mill, whose basic mode of operation is very similar to the whirling lawn sprayers of our own era.

The main design elements of the water turbines used in Britain and Ireland were developed in France, though engineers in Britain, Ireland and the United States made substantial improvements to the pre-existing designs and greatly extended their range. The contribution of Irish engineers was not inconsiderable, the main impetus being provided by Robert Kane who first brought the work of the French engineer, Benöit Fourneyron (1802–67), to an Irish audience in the 1840s. The first Fourneyron reaction turbine to be manufactured in these islands was in MacAdam's Soho Foundry in Belfast, and was installed in Barklie's bleach mill at Mullaghmore, near Coleraine in County Derry, in 1850. At least one contemporary Ulster engineer, James Thomson (1822–92), however, was not content with the mere dissemination of Fourneyron's ideas. As early as 1846, Thomson had developed what he termed a vortex turbine which, in terms of its design characteristics, effectively superseded existing turbines. The first vortex turbine was built in Glasgow and was later installed in a linen beetling mill at Dunadry, County Antrim, in 1852. In 1858, Cork Corporation Water Works which, along with the Corporation Electricity Departments and the Joint Electricity Authority, was responsible for the province's electricity until 1973.

In 1973, the three bodies were amalgamated to form the Northern Ireland Electricity Service (NIES). NIES was a public utility and had four power stations, based at Coolkeeragh, Ballylumford, Kilroot and Belfast. It was responsible for the entire generation, transmission, distribution and supply of electricity throughout Northern Ireland until the spring of 1992, at which time the provision of electricity to the province was privatised.

Northern Ireland reached a total generation capacity of 2,250MW from the four stations, using gas, coal and oil, and is connected to Scotland by an undersea high-voltage 500MW DC cable, which in turn is connected to the ESB network by a 600MW interconnector.

Renewable Energy

Apart from hydro-power sources, considerable efforts have been made in recent years across Ireland to harness other forms of renewable energy, such as wind, tide and biomass. Ireland's first offshore wind project, the Arklow Bank wind park in the Irish Sea, is now in operation. Erection of the project's seven 3.6MW GE machines was completed in only nine weeks. Located around 10km off the east coast on the Arklow Bank, the project's seven GE 3.6 MW wind turbines are the world's first commercial application of offshore wind turbines over 3MW in size. The project is being co-developed by Airtricity and GE Energy.

21

RURAL ELECTRIFICATION

Michael Shiel

THE RURAL ELECTRIFICATION SCHEME (1946–1980) in the Republic of Ireland was the key catalyst in effecting what was called: 'the greatest revolution in Irish rural life since the Land War of the late-Nineteenth and early Twentieth centuries'. The latter had resulted in practically all Irish farmers in the Republic, both large and small, achieving ultimate ownership of their holdings after centuries of near serfdom under mostly alien landlords. There were fewer than 10,000 of these landlords in all — yet they had owned 90 per cent of all farming land in the entire country.

The Shannon Scheme of the late 1920s incorporated the construction of a nationwide transmission and distribution network to supply a high-quality electricity supply to the cities, towns and large villages of Ireland. This had brought many benefits in the form of improved services and communications, the development of industries, and a higher standard of living to the communities, which it served. The vast majority of rural dwellers, however, had not benefited and remained in a poor, backward economy. In too many cases, they were merely existing in social conditions which were, in reality, little more than of a subsistence level. It was obvious that, unless action was taken to remedy this situation, it would remain so, resulting in a widespread 'flight from the land', mostly by the more progressive and active young people, into the cities of Britain and the United States.

The early extension of the supply network to the rural community had been advocated in the original McLaughlin/Siemens proposals to the Free State Government. McLaughlin, in a subsequent address, referred to it as the contribution of modern science and engineering getting to the roots of 'this social evil' (i.e. the 'flight from the land' and the large-scale depopulation of rural Ireland). The outbreak of the Second World War, however, deferred any such extension. Indeed, throughout the duration of the war, the task of maintaining even a basic electricity supply to existing consumers and, in particular, to strategic services and industries was to tax in full the resources — and resourcefulness — of the Electricity Supply Board (ESB).

The wartime Government, however, and in particular the Minister for Industry and Commerce, Sean Lemass,

First Pole being erected in Kilsallaghan in County Dublin in 1944.

regarded rural electrification as a top post-war priority and instructed the ESB to prepare a feasibility report, including costings, to be ready by the end of the war so that the work could commence as soon as materials could be obtained. The first pole of what was to become a nationwide network of well over a million poles was erected in a field in north County Dublin on 5 November 1946.

It was obvious from the beginning that, unless the scheme was subsidised, it would be impossible to extend supply to the vast majority of rural dwellings at acceptable rates of charge. It was finally estimated that, with current costings and based on a 50 per cent capital subsidy from the Government, supply could initially be offered at reasonable rates of charge to 70 per cent of the then-existing 400,000 rural householders, or about 280,000 households. As the scheme progressed and its benefits became apparent, increasing political pressure was put on the Government and the ESB to connect more and more of the 'uneconomic' premises and, by 1980, when the scheme officially came to an end, over 468,000 rural dwellings had been connected. (The larger figure is accounted for by the widespread rural building programme of the late 1960s and 1970s).

In rural Ireland, the vast majority of the rural dwellers (over 95 per cent) lived in isolated houses rather than in villages. This necessitated a large and often meandering 10kV medium-voltage distribution network with single-phase distributors and three-phase 'backbone' feeders, and a preponderance of small-distribution transformers, typically 15kVA, 5kVA, and even 3kVA, supplying from one to ten dwellings at 220V. This system had been successfully used in sparsely populated rural areas in pre-war rural electrification schemes in the United States and in Canada. Initial capital expenditure could be kept down in the early years when demand was low, whilst allowing upgrading simply and cheaply by substituting larger, or adding extra, transformers as demand subsequently built up. The design parameters also allowed for the later raising of the distribution voltage from 10kV to 20kV with minimum network changes. This permitted the general upgrading of large sections of the network where subsequent widespread increase in demand required to be met (as became the case in the 1990s).

It was decided that the unit of development would be the 'area', corresponding closely to the rural 'parish', which was a cohesive social unit. There were approximately 800 rural parishes in the state, each with an area of 25 square miles on average, and containing some 500 households. The order of priority in development depended on factors such as proximity to existing power sources but, in so far as possible, those areas with: (a) the highest percentages of 'acceptances'; and (b) yielding the most economic return on capital investment, would receive priority.

For the scheme to be successful, it would have to attract the cooperation and goodwill of the community, which it was designed to serve by involving the people from the beginning. As a first step, the householders in a parish requesting supply were advised by the ESB to form a local 'Rural Electrification Committee', which would, with the help of ESB personnel, carry out a preliminary canvass of householders. Based on this first poll, a more detailed canvass and a costings exercise were then carried out by ESB officials to determine the order of selection. This close liaison between the community and the ESB staff continued throughout the duration of the scheme and contributed in a big way to the mutual goodwill, which was such a big factor in its success. Differences with landowners regarding pole positions, damage to crops, etc. were usually settled on the spot, rather than become legal issues. In general, the feeling by the community was that this was 'their' scheme, and their cooperation was willingly given.

Because of the nature of the scheme, it was necessary that the overall project management should, for the construction period at least, be kept separate from the other activities of the ESB. Accordingly, the Rural Electrification Office (REO) was set up. Whilst it was autonomous to a considerable degree, it could still access the services of the parent organisation, and would be subject to the same accounting disciplines.

To head this new group, one of the most experienced of the Board's engineers, William Roe — who as one of his outside activities had been an active member of Muintir na Tíre, a nationwide organisation devoted to rural development — was appointed Engineer in Charge. The Board also seconded a number of experienced engineers. These men had successfully contributed to the development of the early ESB supply network and they had, between them, built up a wealth of experience. These included: P.J. Dowling (who was later to succeed Roe as Engineer in Charge) and A.J. McManus (who had, with Dowling and Thomas McLaughlin, prepared the initial report and analysis).

The formation of the actual construction crews involved large-scale recruitment and training of staff from outside: engineers, survey staff, supervisors, charge-hands and semi-skilled and unskilled workers. At peak, there were up to 40 separate construction crews in action. At times, some of these teams would have up to 100 on their staff, giving a total of between 3,500 and 4,000 field staff at any one time.

As it was obvious that most of the engineers would be young graduates, fresh out of engineering school, they required an intense and detailed initial training in 10kV and 220V electricity-network construction specific to the Irish scene. One of the first tasks undertaken by the senior engineers was the preparation of a practical and comprehensive manual of design and construction, based on their own experience. It quickly became famous among the staff as the 'Rural Bible' and was of immense value in ensuring that young engineers were able to shoulder high responsibility and ensure high quality and productivity from the beginning.

Other key staff were recruited from existing ESB staff, and also very many from the pool of ex-army and local defence force officers and non-commissioned officers who were now available as a result of post-war demobilisation. These were well-educated, adaptable, and required very little training to play a full part in supervisory, technical, educational and organisational roles. Unskilled staff (numbering from 40 to 60 upwards in each construction unit) were recruited locally as the unit moved from one area to the next, providing a very welcome source of income to small farmers and to farmers' sons. It also created a strong sense of involvement by the local community.

In parallel with the construction programme went a comprehensive educational and promotional thrust to ensure the widespread acceptance and utilisation of the new power that was essential to the success of the scheme. A special consumer-targeted group of 'Area Organisers' was trained in promoting the acceptance and demonstrating the benefits of the new power, without which the scheme could not be successful, either financially or socially. Throughout the course of the scheme, this group maintained the closest cooperation with the 'consumers-to-be', serving the statutory way-leave notices, explaining, advising, demonstrating, and even persuading the 'initially-reluctant' to take the supply. The vast majority of householders had no experience of electricity, and, initially, needed to have its benefits demonstrated.

The objectives of the scheme received a tremendous boost from close cooperation with the relevant government departments (such as the Department of Agriculture and the Department of Local Government), and with the non-governmental organisations, which were devoted to rural development. The main organisations in this latter category were: The Irish Countrywomen's Association (ICA); Muintir na Tíre; Macra na Feirme; Macra na Tuaithe; the Young Farmers' Clubs; the National Farmers' Association (later to become the 'Irish Farmers Association'); and The Royal Dublin Society, which throughout the whole period of the scheme gave tremendous support to REO at its annual Spring Shows.

Huge efforts on the part of these organisations, in close association with the REO advisory staff, resulted in an outstanding transformation both in the rural economy and in the standard of life in rural areas. By the end of the 1970s, electricity was available to practically every rural household. Running water, indoor toilets and bathrooms, modern cooking, laundry and cleaning methods, television and, increasingly, the telephone, had relieved the rural housewife of the traditional drudgery associated with rural living. Now, rural householders could avail of all the amenities hitherto available only to their urban cousins. On the farm, innovations such as: farmyard lighting, milking machines, stock watering, improved dairy hygiene, milk cooling, motive power for milking, and fodder processing all contributed to an increase in production levels and in quality of output, in order to avail of the huge new markets opening up in mainland Europe.

By the end of March 1980, the scheme had been officially completed and absorbed into the general management and administration of the ESB Over one million poles, 100,000km of lines and some 1,001,000 transformers had been erected. Over 468,000 rural dwellings, farms and businesses, or 99 per cent of all premises had been connected to the national electricity network. In the 34-year period (1946–1980), the total cost of the scheme amounted to £109 million (including network reinforcement over the years, as demand grew). The total government subsidy was £29.7 million, or 25 per cent of the overall capital cost. The balance was provided by the ESB out of the combined Urban/Rural income.

22

EARLY INDUSTRIES IN IRELAND

Colin Rynne

THE PROGRESS OF TRULY LARGE-SCALE INDUSTRIALISATION in Ireland in the nineteenth century exhibits a pronounced regional bias, with British levels of industrialisation being experienced only in the counties and towns of Armagh, Antrim, Down, Londonderry, Tyrone, Belfast and Carrickfergus, and in certain ports such as Drogheda. The province of Ulster, in general, faced the same resource constraints as the rest of the island, yet it proved more adept at developing successful forms of regional specialisation within the economy of the United Kingdom.

The growing of flax was well suited to this region of generally poor soils, but with a mild climate and small-scale cropping patterns. The low profitably of Ulster farms compelled local landlords to find other means of increasing their incomes, and, to this end, new tenants with weaving skills began to receive more favourable treatment. In the late seventeenth century, fine linens remained the only important goods that an increasingly self-sufficient British economy still needed to import. Tariffs on continental linens were consequently increased, whilst import duties on Irish and Scottish linens exported to Britain were removed in 1696. The evolution of the Ulster linen industry, therefore, exhibits all of the principal characteristics of proto-industrialisation and was eventually transformed into a factory-based industry. Linen manufacturers imitated the modus operandi of the Belfast cotton mills and, after the latter's decline, became the main textile industry in eastern Ulster during the 1820s, and thereafter the largest of its type in the world.

In the rest of Ireland, attempts at regional specialisation were less successful — often spectacularly so — and industrial development remained well below the European norm. In the period 1730–75, the rapid development of the British Atlantic economy brought with it an increased demand for Irish agricultural produce, and the Irish economy, working to its strengths, adjusted to accommodate it. This specialisation brought about a general change from tillage to pasture, and the provision trade began to enjoy considerable success in the port cities of Dublin, Cork and Waterford. Thereafter Ireland's most successful early industries in the south of the country included brewing, distilling and grain milling.

The Consolidation Phase, 1978–1986

Many of the firms from abroad that were setting up in Ireland created a demand for professional engineers. Shortages of graduate engineers were experienced, and the IEI led a campaign to increase the capacity of the third-level institutions, to ensure that supply matched demand.

The first two years of this phase were dominated by the decision of the Irish Government to join the European Monetary System. The great majority of industries in Ireland favoured this approach, on condition that a safety net could be assured in the event of a significant devaluation of sterling against the Irish pound. As part of the arrangement negotiated by the Government with the EC, a substantial loan at a subsidised interest rate was made available for the purpose of modernising Ireland's telecommunications infrastructure.

At this time, the Commission expressed its unease about the distortion of competition arising from the different treatment given by the Irish Government to profits earned from the export of manufactured products and those sold on the home market. After protracted negotiations, the Government agreed that all manufacturing profits would be taxed at ten per cent.

During this consolidation phase, the impact of operating in a customs-free zone of 280 million people took some time to take effect. The trend that had been established during the transition phase continued. New industries from abroad were attracted to Ireland in increasing numbers. Newcomers during this phase included Apple, Microsoft and Schering Plough. There were now over 800 overseas-owned companies in Ireland, of which over one-third were US-owned. High-technology industries, such as computers, microelectronics, and pharmaceutical and organic chemicals industries, sustained a 15 per cent annual rate of expansion and, by 1986, accounted for over 40 per cent of total manufacturing output. At the end of the period, the great majority of firms that were incapable of surviving in free-trade conditions had disappeared.

Despite these difficulties, the overall growth of manufacturing industry during this consolidation phase was sustained at five per cent per annum. Once again, the expansion of new foreign industries more than compensated for the decline of traditional sectors.

Irish industry continued to diversify its export markets, and the United Kingdom's share of Irish exports fell to 35 per cent, whilst the share of continental member states rose to 35 per cent. Then, in 1986, Spain and Portugal joined the EC, amid concerns that labour-intensive industry might be attracted to these countries rather than Ireland.

Expansion Phase, 1987–1992

This period commenced with the passage of the Single European Act, which would create a genuine Single Internal Market by adopting a programme to implement the recommendations of the 1985 White Paper. Apart from an acceptance of the logic of the Single Market, there was an enlightened self-interest by Irish industry in supporting the proposed Act. Industry in Ireland was exporting over 70 per cent of its output, mainly to other member states. It was therefore far more interested in having free access to this large market than in protecting a very limited home market.

Despite the disruption to international trade caused by the Gulf War in 1991 and the currency crisis of 1992, the rate of growth in the output of Irish manufacturing industry accelerated to an average of eight per cent per annum during this period. The flow of new industries from abroad continued unabated. Intel, Dell and Sandoz (Novartis) established

The International Financial Services Centre, Dublin.

substantial operations, and the output of computers and pharmaceuticals maintained a growth rate of some 15 per cent per annum; the food-processing sector showed a sustained steady expansion of about three per cent per annum; and, for the first time, the traditional sectors of industry showed a marked increase of some five per cent per annum. This performance provided the clearest indication yet that almost all of Irish industry was now competitive and capable of growing in a large single market of almost 300 million people. The structure of the industrial base was now sound, and a continuation of the same broad policies seemed the best way forward. In addition, the innovative establishment of the International Financial Services Centre (IFSC) in the Dublin docklands, with a favourable corporate tax regime agreed with the EC, was having a significant impact towards the end of this phase.

The completion of the Single European Market in 1992 had an important side effect on the island of Ireland. All customs posts were to be removed between member states, and this included their removal at the border between the Republic and Northern Ireland. By the end of this period, Irish exports to other EU countries (43 per cent) exceeded exports to the United Kingdom (31 per cent) for the first time.

The Celtic Tiger Phase, 1993–2001

The Maastricht Treaty in 1992 set the wheels in motion for economic and monetary union throughout what was now called the European Union (EU). Prospective participating member states were required to manage their economies so that inflation rates, exchequer borrowing, public debt, and interest rates would converge towards specific targets. A common currency, the Euro, would be introduced, and exchange-rate parities with the Euro would be set irrevocably at the end of 1998. Industry in Ireland was enthusiastically in favour. Irish industry had consistently welcomed the expansion of the EU. Ireland's role, like that of any other region of the EU, was to be a specialist supplier of those goods and services for which it enjoys a comparative advantage. The excellence of the Irish education system was fundamental to success.

The high-technology industries accelerated their average annual rate of increase in output to 27 per cent. In 2001, they accounted for almost 60 per cent of the value of manufacturing output; the food and drinks processing and the traditional industries continued to grow at a moderate pace. The total output of manufacturing industry had increased by 12 per cent per annum over the period. Industry strengthened its position as the key driver of economic growth. New names such as Hewlett-Packard, Compaq and Wyeth Biopharma joined the growing throng of foreign direct-investment companies.

The diversification of Ireland's trade has continued unabated. Other member states of the EU (including the UK) account for over 60 per cent of Irish exports, and the United States about 20 per cent. The enlargement of the Union in 1995 brought the total population to 340 million. Trade is now likely to develop most rapidly with the Euroland member states, as there is no currency risk.

Irish manufacturing production is concentrated in four broad product groups: organic chemicals and pharmaceuticals, computers, electrical machinery and scientific apparatus, which together account for 72 per cent of Irish exports, and have doubled their share in the past decade. These sectors are dominated by engineering professionals. In addition, there is a strong reliance on information technology in the international and financial trading sector, which now employs over 40 per cent as many as manufacturing industry.

In the latter half of this period, the European Commission returned to the issue of the distorting effect of Ireland's different rate of corporate profits taxation for manufacturing and internationally traded service, compared to the much higher rate charged on other businesses in Ireland. Finally, in August 1998, the Commission agreed to the gradual phasing in of a 12.5 per cent tax rate by 2003 for all businesses. The Commission accepted that differences in corporate taxation rates between member states do not fall within the definition of state aid.

The remarkable developments of recent years have required a very substantial input from the engineering profession. Over three per cent of the workforce describe themselves as engineers. Society has become more technology oriented. It is no coincidence that at least 20 of the chief executives of the top 100 companies operating in the Republic are professional engineers.

Infrastructure

For many decades, the key constraint on economic development had been an underdeveloped industrial sector. The rapid rate of industrial expansion during the 1990s resulted in a doubling of the total output of the economy during the decade. There were now some 1,200 overseas-owned companies operating in the Republic; income per capita had exceeded the EU average; unemployment had fallen to 3.5 per cent; and the population was growing at more than one per cent per annum with considerable assistance from immigration.

However, infrastructural constraints began to emerge in areas such as transport, energy and housing. These were

The Fab24 facility at INTEL in Leixlip, County Dublin.

most severe in the Dublin area where population growth was most rapid. A similar, though less-pronounced, imbalance in population growth was evident in Northern Ireland, particularly in the Belfast area.

A programme to build 900km of motorways/ high-quality dual-carriageways between Dublin and the five main urban centres is currently underway in line with government objectives. These urban highways are being built in response to projected needs based on the extrapolation of historic traffic volumes.

A substantial programme of rail permanent-way and rolling-stock upgrading has been ongoing in recent years. Speeds of 150kph are now achievable on improved sections of the Belfast to Dublin, and Dublin to Cork routes. Two lines of a rapid transit system (Luas) are now operational in Dublin. A proposed new Metro for Dublin City, scheduled for possible completion by 2010, and comprising about 60km of line, will be the largest single public-transport project over the next decade.

Over 20 million passengers now travel through Irish airports. Air travel has been growing at the rate of ten per cent per annum over the past decade. Traffic to and from regional airports is increasing more rapidly, and is now at a record level. Further expansion of airport facilities is planned.

Over eight million passengers now travel by sea annually, and more than 57 million tonnes of freight are transported. Freight traffic through Dublin Port has trebled in the past eight years. The largest vehicle and passenger ferry in the world sails daily between Dublin and Holyhead.

There are around 300km of natural gas pipeline on the island. Demand is expected to double by the end of the decade. It is anticipated that the Corrib gas field off the west coast will replace the indigenous gas supply provided by the Kinsale gas field.

Electricity demand is forecast to increase by five per cent per annum over the next decade. This will require the construction of close to 300MW capacity per year to achieve an adequate reserve.

Information technology has transformed society over the past decade. It has meant the death of distance, and reduced the disadvantages of our island location.

Some of the largest companies in the world, such as Microsoft, Hewlett-Packard, IBM and Intel, have production operations in Ireland. A universally accessible broadband network is being installed, together with very high-speed

In the late 1840s, the Belfast Harbour Commissioners appointed William Dargan to construct a channel to straighten the course of the River Lagan and improve access to the town for the ever-increasing size of vessels using the port. The spoil was deposited on slob land on the County Down side of the river, to create Dargan's Island — later renamed Queen's Island when Queen Victoria opened the new channel in 1849. In 1853, a shipyard was established on part of this new ground and let to a Robert Hickson, who operated an iron foundry in Eliza Street. The new shipyard, which was to concentrate on iron ships, was intended to provide a use for the product of the iron foundry. In 1854, Edward Harland was appointed manager of this yard, and he purchased it in 1858. The first order under his ownership was for three ships for the Bibby Line and the successful completion of *Venetian, Sicilian* and *Syrian* brought further orders. Gustav Wolff, who had been in charge of the drawing office since 1858, joined Harland as a partner in 1861. From there, progress was rapid and the firm gained a reputation for innovation in ship design — in particular, designs which increased the carrying capacity of ships without increasing the power required to propel them. The iron ships were treated as box-girder designs with flat bottoms, which became known as 'Belfast bottoms', the design being copied by many other shipbuilders. The construction of *Oceanic* in 1870 for the Ocean Steam Navigation Company led to a long association of the shipyard with the White Star Line. *Oceanic* introduced new standards of accommodation, comfort, style and speed for the prestige passenger route across the North Atlantic, and also mechanical innovations to increase speed and reduce costs for the owners. Such large ships needed regular refurbishment of the shipyard, and massive investment in new facilities became a constant feature of Harland & Wolff over the years.

By 1884, both Harland and Wolff were pursuing other interests and felt the need to reduce their involvement in the business, Therefore, they took on three further partners who had been premium apprentices with the firm — W.J. Pirrie, W.H. Wilson and his brother, A.B. Wilson. The latter left in 1885 to manage the old established firm of John Rowan & Son, a supplier to Harland & Wolff. Walter Wilson was the naval architect responsible for designing the ships that Pirrie built and sold. The firm officially became a limited liability company in December 1885 as 'The Queen's Island Shipbuilding and Engineering Company Limited'. In 1888, the name was changed to Harland & Wolff Limited. At the same time, the works were refitted with new machinery capable of handling the increased size of plates available from the iron founders who were now using open-hearth steel-making plant.

In June 1896, the yard suffered a serious fire that started in the woodworking area and which destroyed a great part of the south yard and the adjacent engine works of Workman Clark. The opportunity was taken to expand the facilities to cope with the rapidly increasing size of vessels that were being ordered. As a result, the new No. 2 berth was built to the north side of the existing facilities, capable of holding a ship of 700 feet by 70 feet. The main innovation of this berth was the gigantic gantry around 100 feet high, which carried mobile, hydraulically operated, cranes for lifting the ever-increasing size of plates. They also carried the hydraulic riveting machines, which were required

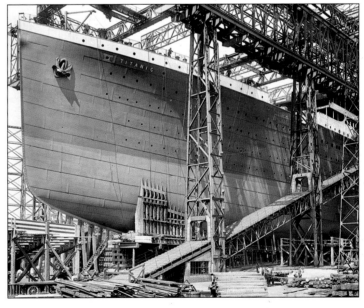

Harland & Wolff North Yard with 'Titanic' prior to launch (1911).

Harland & Wolff Engine Works erecting shop with reciprocating engine for 'Britannic' (1929).

to speed up production generally and, in particular, to deal with the double bottoms that were a standard feature of vessels built by Harland & Wolff. It is believed that Pirrie based the system on that at the Newport Mews yard in the United States. A new building, the Alexandra Docks Works, was constructed for the repair department, which was growing as fast as the main business.

Harland & Wolff had opened its own engine shop in 1881 and had led the way in developing triple-expansion steam engines. Amalgamation with the John Brown Company of Glasgow in 1907 led to the acquisition of a licence to build Parsons steam turbines, and these were used in conjunction with reciprocating engines to power the *Olympic*-class ships. As steam power reached the peak of its efficiency, the diesel engine became more practical and offered more potential. In 1912, Pirrie formed a joint company with the Danish company Burmeister & Wain, which had developed a reliable marine version. Over the next 40 years or so, the engine works of Harland & Wolff, under the guidance of Sir Frederick Rebbeck and later C.C. Pounder, produced outstanding developments in double-acting two- and four-stroke engines and opposed piston engines. As well as the marine versions, these engines were used in electrical generating plant and for other industrial purposes. Smaller versions were available and were later used to power railway locomotives for Irish and Brazilian railways.

During the First World War, there was a change from reliance on commercial to admiralty contracts and the company used its woodworking skills to build aircraft for the Avro, de Havilland and Handley Page companies. After the war, there followed a short boom period during which tonnage lost in the war was replaced. Following the death of Lord Pirrie in 1924, the firm struggled on through the world depression, but was brought back to prominence by Sir Frederick Rebbeck and built some memorable vessels including *HMS Belfast* and *RMS Andes* prior to the Second World War. During the war, Harland & Wolff built a range of vessels for the Admiralty and the Ministry of War Transport, from tank landing craft to aircraft carriers, the last of which, *HMS Eagle*, was launched in 1946. Again the company diversified and built tanks and aircraft fuselages, the latter in conjunction with the subsidiary company, Short Brothers & Harland. After the war, for three years, 1946–48, Harland & Wolff led the world league of shipyard output. In the 1950s and 1960s, the company still led the way with the innovative design of *Southern Cross* and *Canberra*, but under government ownership reinvestment fell drastically. A series of very large cargo carriers of up to 170,000 tons displacement was built for transporting oil, LPG or bulk cargoes, together with *Sea Quest*, an oil-drilling platform which found the North Sea oil reserves, and a pioneering SWOPS (single well oil-producing system) vessel. At the end of the twentieth century, privatisation, reduction in government aid and international competition had reached the point where the company could no longer compete effectively and the old firm of Harland & Wolff was reduced to a shadow of its former glory.

In 1879, Frank Workman founded the firm of Workman, Clark & Co. He was joined by George S. Clark in 1880, also a former premium apprentice with Harland & Wolff, and, in 1891, by Charles E. Allan, whose family owned the

25

THE IRISH PEAT INDUSTRY

Finbar Callanan

Early Developments

The commercial exploitation of peat resources has a long history. Over the centuries, many Continental countries evaluated the various uses of their considerable peat resources, often with particular emphasis on carbonisation for use in metallurgy. In Ireland, with an estimated 3,000,000 acres of peat cover, there was also considerable interest in the development of this exceptional national resource, not only from the point of view of reclamation, but also for the production of peat fuel for domestic and industrial use. In 1809, a commission on the bogs of Ireland was established, its prime purpose being to examine their potential reclamation. The engineers who, along with teams of surveyors, carried out the relevant surveys included Richard Griffith, later to become President of the Institution of Engineers of Ireland, and Alexander Nimmo, one of the most eminent civil engineers working in Ireland at that time.

The Bog Commission reported on over 2,800,000 acres, of which about 60 per cent was 'flat red bog' and the remainder 'covering of mountains'. Drainage patterns were designed and detailed reclamation proposals made and costed. The reports and the associated maps and proposals that were prepared over a period of five years were a very significant achievement. They were the first physical and qualitative survey of Ireland's peat lands and formed a compendium of knowledge with regard to current thinking on the drainage and reclamation of peat. However many problems were to arise with regard to the implementation of the report, varying from the potential costs involved, the ownership of the bogs in question, as well as the lack of an overall governmental will to carry out such a large scale and costly enterprise. Apart from limited reclamation, mainly on the fringes of the greater peat deposits, little was achieved. The reports, however, were to form an invaluable source of reference in subsequent years.

By the 1840s, the use of peat as a fuel still exercised the minds of many entrepreneurs. In *The Industrial Resources of Ireland*, published in 1844, Sir Robert Kane wrote 'There is nothing in the industrialised economy of this country which requires more attention than the collection and preparation of our turf. Indeed I may say, that for practical purposes this valuable fuel is absolutely spoiled as it is now prepared'. Kane went on to detail the various means by which experimenters had produced forms of densified turf using mechanical and other processes 'to remove the porosity and elasticity of turf so that it may assume the solidity of coal'.

It is interesting to note that the first paper published in volume one of the *Transactions of The Institution of Civil Engineers of Ireland* (1845) was 'On the Artificial Preparation of Turf, independently of season or weather' by Robert Mallet. The index to the transactions lists a number of papers on the subject of peat extraction and utilisation, published during the nineteenth and twentieth centuries, all of which added to the quantum of knowledge and interest leading to the major developments of the twentieth century.

In his paper to the IEI Heritage Society on 'The Development of the Peat Industry after Kane, 1850-1950', published in 2002, James Martin listed the many attempts made 'by some of our best engineers, entrepreneurs and political brains' to exploit this great natural resource. It was noted that peat was used in a variety of applications as a fuel for domestic, industrial and transport purposes, in carbonised form in manufacturing processes, for the production of peat gas for lighting and, more successfully, as litter for the bedding of animals, as a soil conditioner, and for sanitary purposes. There was constant competition from coal and the lack of capital, the cost of development, the variability of the weather and fluctuating demand severely inhibited, and was indeed, became the ruin of many enterprising initiatives.

The value of maceration of raw peat to break down its colloidal structure as an aid to drying and densification was well known on the Continent and in parts of Ireland, but densification by the drying of powdered peat to form briquettes by mechanical compression was a constant goal of a number of entrepreneurs, who saw it as a method of mechanised production that would allow peat to compete economically with coal.

Charles Hodgson and Briquetting

Following some earlier experience, Charles Hodgson in the 1850s developed a method for milling peat and turning it into briquettes, a technique not unlike that used today on a larger scale. Hodgson's installation was at Derrylea, near Portarlington in County Laois. This system involved harrowing the bog surface on dry days with a series of pin harrows drawn by a steam-driven engine that pulverised the bog surface to a depth of a half inch or so and, after repeated harrowings, the peat mull was harvested at 55 per cent moisture content. This mull was then dried by a series of boilers to a moisture content of 10 per cent and compressed into peat briquettes to be sold on the Dublin market. This plant was in production for just three years and, while technically it was very sophisticated for its time, it was forced to close for financial reasons.

Early Nineteenth Century

In subsequent decades, other enterprises were founded and floundered, but the idea of utilising Ireland's peat resources continued to be a matter of considerable interest, not only to enterprising individuals, but also to government. In 1917, an Irish Peat Enquiry Sub-Committee was established by the Department of Agriculture & Technical Instruction, amongst its members being Sir John Purser Griffith and Professor Pierce Purcell (Professor of Civil Engineering at UCD). It's remit was to 'inquire into, and consider the experiences already gained in Ireland in respect of the winning, preparation and use of peat for fuel and for other purposes and to suggest what means shall be taken to ascertain the conditions under which in the most favourably situated localities it can be profitably won, prepared and used, having regard to the economic destined for Ferbane and Rhode, were in the design stage when the decision was made by BnaM to switch its major future development from sod peat to milled peat for power generation. This was not a decision welcomed by the ESB, who were seriously concerned by the economics of peat for power generation compared to other fuels. However the Government, led by the then Taoiseach Sean Lemass, and ably supported by the Minister for Foreign Affairs, Frank Aiken, declared itself very much in favour of the large-scale utilisation of the

Harvesting milled peat.

country's peat resources by the fully mechanised milled peat system. The change over to milled peat commenced with the drainage patterns on those bogs already in development for sod peat being changed to the milled peat system. Thus commenced the Board's Second Development Programme, which was to lead to considerable expansion in development of milled peat harvesting. The 20,000 acre (8,000ha) Boora group of bogs was the first to make the change over and, in 1953, construction commenced on the power station at Ferbane, which was to take its supplies of milled peat from Boora Bog. This station's first generating set was commissioned in 1956 and others were to follow.

The Briquette Factories

However, in 1956, the ESB announced that they were cutting back on plans for increased electricity output. This decision seriously affected the development plans of BnaM. At that stage the government decided that the surplus of peat now be- coming available should be used to feed two briquette factories, at Croghan and Derrinlough in County Offaly, and work commenced on the two factories, each with a capacity of 100,000 tons per annum. With the capacity of Lullymore having been increased to 50,000 tons per annum, the total designed annual production was 250,000 tons per annum, which with substantial improvements in productivity was to be greatly exceeded in subsequent years. Peat briquettes proved to be a popular and invaluable addition to the industrial and domestic fuel market.

Also during the late 1950s, the ESB, at the behest of the Government, commissioned four 5MW generating stations in the west of Ireland to burn sod peat (hand won and machine won) produced locally by private suppliers. Stations were built at Cahirciveen, County Kerry, Milltown Malbay, County Clare, Screeb, County Galway and at Gweedore County Donegal. BnaM were not involved in these developments, which were conceived primarily as an economic boost to the areas in question.

The Organisation Expands

The following decades saw a considerable expansion of the milled peat programme with the completion of power stations at Rhode, Lanesboro, Shannonbridge and Bellacorick, and the extension to the station at Ferbane. By 1968/69, the proportion of total electricity produced from BnaM peat had reached 36 per cent. That did not mean that the 1960s were an easy period for the production of milled peat, as a succession of bad summers early in the decade caused great difficulty in the harvesting of milled peat. In addition Hurricane Debbie in 1961 did immense damage to the stockpiles of milled peat and caused a complete re-think on the protection of all the Board's stocks from wind and rain. This led to the widespread and highly successful use of polythene sheeting to protect all stockpiles, a practice which not only protected milled peat from storm damage but also significantly guarded against any increase in the moisture content of the finished product, whether milled, sod or moss peat.

Technological Advances

One attempted solution for the maintenance of security of supply from the milled peat bogs was the development of the Foidin machine that travelled the milled peat fields feeding surface peat into a macerator and laying a carpet of small sod turf behind it, which would dry rapidly and be less susceptible to the vagaries of the weather. It was a system, which for some time showed promise until other problems arose that led eventually to this imaginatively designed mechanical system being abandoned in favour of remaining with the traditional milled peat system.

From the commencement of the First Programme, there was a constant improvement in the design of the milled peat winning machinery, with significant improvements in the output of drainage, milling, harrowing, ridging, and harvesting machines. Many of these improvements originated at work level and drew on the wide experience gained in operations, where the imperative had to be to avail of every available period of air drying during the summer harvesting period. This innovative approach toward the continuous re-design and improvement of milled peat harvesting machines and techniques has continued to the present time.

It was recognized early on that the surest way to achieve security of supply was to increase acreage under production and to move from the original design target of 100 tons per net acre to a target of 70 tons per net acre (a net acre representing the actual acreage from which milled peat was produced). This was achieved by gradually acquiring and developing over a period of years the peripheral areas of high bog and cutaway that had not been considered in the original acquisitions and other areas that had been cut over by hand winning in previous centuries.

But it was not only in milled peat and briquetting that considerable technological advances were made. Whilst the production of sod peat involved a fully mechanised and highly effective excavation, maceration and spreading system, the subsequent harvesting of the drying peat sods involved a significant proportion of hand work to place the sods in footings ('elevate to ventilate') from which they could be mechanically collected and transferred to the stock piles. A German tracked machine, known as 'The Hedgehog' had been developed that, with a series of spiked wheels in front, lifted the sods off the spread and placed them in windrows for drying. This system was successful for up to 50 per cent of the crop. However in 1960, a plough attachment fitted to the front of a tracked tractor was developed at Ballydermot works that, for a minimal cost, could perform the windrowing procedure at four times the output of the German machine. This Irish attachment was imitated widely on the Continent in other peat enterprises and showed how an and a considerably reduced maintenance requirement, with only eleven greasing points compared with the then more normal 80. Unfortunately, the First World War put paid to production plans. One prototype was exhibited at the New York motor show of 1916 but any thoughts of production in America had to be shelved due to the war effort and the subsequent Depression of 1921

Ford Motor Company

The Ford family emigrated from West Cork in 1847 and settled into farming at Dearborn in Michigan. Henry Ford was born into this family in 1863 and, from an early age, developed an antipathy to what he saw as the drudgery and hard labour of farming. His dream was to mechanise farming and also to provide an automobile for personal transport.

By 1896, he had built his first car and, in 1906, was the biggest car manufacturer in America, with a total of 8,729 Fords produced in that year. The Model T, which was specifically designed for ease and simplicity of operation, maintenance and repair, answered the motoring needs of an era, and a total of 15 million were produced between 1909 and 1927.

The First World War, and the consequent shortage of farm labour, stimulated the mechanisation of farming, and Henry Ford decided to build a factory in Cork, dedicated to the manufacture of tractors. The massive new Marina plant covering 330,000 square feet on a site of 136 acres was commissioned in 1919, and the first Fordson tractor came off the production line on 3 July of that year.

The Ford Factory at Marina, Cork, in the early 1960s.

Cortina assembly at Cork in 1967.

Following the establishment of the Irish Free State in 1922, the British Government imposed a substantial duty on imports of Irish parts into the UK. This necessitated the building of a new Ford factory at Dagenham, which took a few years to achieve so that Cork got a temporary reprieve. And so, in the event, a mixture of parts and tractor manufacture and Model-T manufacture for the Irish market kept the Marina plant busy up to 1927.

The Model T was followed by the Model A, and Cork was commissioned to build a special 14.9hp small-bore engine to minimise car tax in countries where duties were based on engine capacity. Some 6,394 of these AF engines were manufactured in Cork in 1928 for worldwide markets.

The manufacture of tractors was again concentrated in Cork in 1929 and 1930, with 25,000 being made, mainly for export. The world economic depression of the early 1930s, together with tariff barriers on Irish/English trade, made life very difficult. Tractor production was transferred to Dagenham in 1934, and many of the Irish workers went with it. From then on, Cork served as an assembly plant for the Irish market.

Crossle Car Company

For some 45 years, the Crossle Car Co. operated by the partnership of John Crossle and Ernie Black, has been supplying race-winning cars to match the various Formulae categories in Europe and America. They have been a nursery to many